# ROUTLEDGE LIBRARY EDITIONS: KUWAIT

Volume 5

# THE MANPOWER PROBLEM IN KUWAIT

# THE MANPOWER PROBLEM
# IN KUWAIT

SHAMLAN Y. ALESSA

**R** Routledge
Taylor & Francis Group

LONDON AND NEW YORK

First published in 1981 by Kegan Paul International Ltd

This edition first published in 2018
by Routledge
2 Park Square, Milton Park, Abingdon, Oxon OX14 4RN

and by Routledge
711 Third Avenue, New York, NY 10017

*Routledge is an imprint of the Taylor & Francis Group, an informa business*

*British Library Cataloguing in Publication Data*
A catalogue record for this book is available from the British Library

ISBN: 978-1-138-62956-1 (Set)
ISBN: 978-1-315-15946-1 (Set) (ebk)
ISBN: 978-1-138-06535-2 (Volume 5) (hbk)
ISBN: 978-1-138-06550-5 (Volume 5) (pbk)
ISBN: 978-1-315-15970-6 (Volume 5) (ebk)

**Publisher's Note**
The publisher has gone to great lengths to ensure the quality of this reprint but points out that some imperfections in the original copies may be apparent.

**Disclaimer**
The publisher has made every effort to trace copyright holders and would welcome correspondence from those they have been unable to trace.

# The manpower problem in Kuwait

Shamlan Y. Alessa

Kegan Paul International
London and Boston

First published in 1981
by Kegan Paul International Ltd
39 Store Street,
London WC1E 7DD,
9 Park Street,
Boston, Mass. 02108, USA and
Broadway House,
Newtown Road,
Henley-on-Thames,
Oxon RG9 1EN
Set in Press Roman by
Hope Services, Abingdon, Oxon.
and printed in Great Britain by
Biddles Ltd, Guildford

British Library Cataloguing in Publication Data

Alessa, Shamlan Y.
The manpower problem in Kuwait. — (Arab world studies)
1. Labor supply — Kuwait
2. Kuwait — Economic conditions
I. Title II. Series
331.11'09536705   HD5836.K/

ISBN 0-7103-0009-3

To the memory of my father,
the most influential person in my life,
who in 1911 opened the first school in Kuwait
and inspired in me the pursuit of knowledge

# Contents

Acknowledgments                                        xi

Introduction                                          xiii

1  Pre-oil Kuwait                                        1

   Geography                                            1
   People                                               1
   The economy                                          3
   Summary                                              8

2  Manpower in Kuwait                                   10

   Kuwait's economy after the discovery of oil         10
   Population and the labor force                       11
   The labor force in Kuwait                            16
   Distribution of the labor force by economic sector   18
   Distribution of the labor force by major occupational group  21
   Distribution of the labor force according to educational
       attainment                                       27
   Summary                                              29

3  Foreign manpower                                     31

   The pull factor                                      31
   The push factor                                      33
   Profile of the foreign labor force in Kuwait         39
   Legal and economic conditions of the foreign labor force  43
   Uncertainty in Kuwait                                50
   Summary                                              54

# Contents

4  Education and manpower                              56

    Higher education                                   63
    Problem of teachers                                69
    Vocational and technical education                 71
    Vocational training in the oil sector              79
    Summary                                            81

5  Toward manpower planning in Kuwait                  88

    Reforming the civil service                        89
    Reforming the educational system                   95
    Vocational and technical education                 97
    Women's participation in the labor force           99
    Reforming the Nationality Law                     106
    Manpower Center                                    111
    Organization of the Center                         113
    Summary                                            116

    Notes                                              117

    Bibliography                                       128

    Index                                              134

# Tables

| 2.1 | Import figures and oil revenue, 1954–80 | 12 |
|---|---|---|
| 2.2 | Population growth, by sex and major population group | 13 |
| 2.3 | Distribution of population by age group | 14 |
| 2.4 | Labor force, by nationality and participation rate | 17 |
| 2.5 | Labor force, by economic sector, 1975 | 19 |
| 2.6 | Labor force, by major occupational group, 1970, 1975 | 22 |
| 2.7 | Selected professional and scientific occupations, by sex and nationality, 1975 | 23 |
| 2.8 | Ministry of Education administrative staff, 1977–8 | 25 |
| 2.9 | Technicians, skilled and semi-skilled workers, 1975 | 26 |
| 2.10 | Distribution of labor force according to educational attainment | 28 |
| 3.1 | Palestinian and Jordanian population in Kuwait, census years 1957–75 | 34 |
| 3.2 | Egyptian population in Kuwait, census years 1957–75 | 35 |
| 3.3 | Iraqi population in Kuwait, census years 1957–75 | 37 |
| 3.4 | Iranian population in Kuwait, census years 1957–75 | 38 |
| 3.5 | Population of Kuwait by sex and nationality, 1975 | 39 |
| 3.6 | Foreign labor force and median stay in Kuwait, by nationality | 40 |
| 3.7 | Non-Kuwaiti labor force, by nationality and major occupational group | 42 |
| 3.8 | Average government salary | 45 |
| 4.1 | Number of students and teachers in public schools | 58 |
| 4.2 | Number of teachers, by nationality and sex | 59 |
| 4.3 | Non-Kuwaiti students in public schools | 61 |
| 4.4 | Number of Palestinian schools, classrooms, teachers and students | 62 |

*Tables*

| | | |
|---|---|---|
| 4.5 | Number of government schools, classrooms, teachers and students, by sex and level of education | 64 |
| 4.6 | Cost per annum of each student in school, 1974-5 | 66 |
| 4.7 | Students attending university abroad, by country and sex | 67 |
| 4.8 | Number of Kuwait University students, by field of study, sex and nationality, 1975-6 | 68 |
| 4.9 | Number of teachers at all levels (except university) by sex and nationality, 1976-9 | 70 |
| 4.10 | Kuwait University MA and PhD scholarships, by country of destination, 1978-9 | 71 |
| 4.11 | School for Vocational Training of Labor: numbers enlisted and specialization, 1955-8 | 72 |
| 4.12 | Industrial College, number of graduates, 1957-74 | 73 |
| 4.13 | Organized training by ministry, number of students and required certificate, 1973 | 74 |
| 4.14 | Job training, 1972 | 76 |
| 4.15 | Cost of vocational and educational training | 76 |
| 4.16 | Relative distribution of workers by occupation in six companies | 78 |
| 4.17 | Employment in the oil companies, 1961, 1971 | 80 |
| 4.18 | Distribution of employees according to occupation (12 years and more), 1970 | 82 |
| 4.19 | Illiterate population in census years 1957, 1961, 1965, 1970, 1975 | 84 |
| 4.20 | Total enrollment in adult education programs, 1976-9 | 85 |
| 4.21 | College graduates for academic years, 1974-80 | 86 |
| 5.1 | Government civil servants by educational attainment, 1976 | 89 |
| 5.2 | Salaries and wages in the government sector, 1965-75 | 92 |
| 5.3 | Women in the labor force, by nationality and participation rate | 100 |
| 5.4 | Preference for government jobs | 101 |
| 5.5 | Population and labor force, 1980-1 | 107 |

# Acknowledgments

No words can express the deep gratitude I owe to all those people connected, directly and indirectly, with the writing of this book.

Many thanks are due to the numerous people who took it upon themselves to assist me in the monumental task of gathering all the available and accessible data relating to manpower in Kuwait, especially the Ministry of Planning and the Arab Planning Institute.

Most of all I am extremely grateful to Professors Arpad von Lazar and Robert Meagher, two very great friends and advisers, who throughout gave unstinting support and assistance.

Finally, I would like to thank my wife for all her help and support during the writing of this book.

# Introduction

Development, or modernization, has become one of the most fascinating topics of study for social scientists from a variety of backgrounds. Although scholars disagree on any single definition of development, it cannot be said to take place without an improvement in the condition and well-being of man. The development of such human resources is essential for sustained economic growth. As one economist has stated: 'The country that can not develop its people can develop little else.'[1] The availability of trained manpower is essential for the success of any socio-economic development program. Human resources, in any country, represent the fundamental factor of its development, but development and the success of a human-resources program depend greatly on the existing political and social system. Thus economic growth not only requires adequate manpower but also a change in people's social and political outlook, as Eugene Staley pointed out:[2]

> If capital investment and material technology are pushed energetically in an underdeveloped country while little or no attention is given to the deliberate promotion of appropriate social and psychological change — that is, to the more specifically human side of development — the result is likely to be either a failure of the development process to 'take' and become self-generating or creation of a menace to the Free World.

It is clear that the manpower issue is not purely an economic one but rather a multidisciplinary one, involving sociology, psychology, economics, law and political science.

There is an abundance of literature on underdeveloped countries where the emphasis is on capital shortage and surplus of labour as the impediments to economic growth. There are very few studies, however,

*Introduction*

where surplus of capital and shortage of labor (manpower) are the problem. Kuwait is just such a case and as such represents in many respects the opposite of the less developed countries in general. It presents unique problems through its unusual combination of capital surplus but scarcity of indigenous labor, both skilled and unskilled.

The manpower problem in Kuwait cannot be adequately understood in economic terms alone, as we have seen. The issue has rather to be seen as a combination of economic, social and political factors. We can isolate these as follows:

(1) A predominance of expatriate labor. The rapid growth in Kuwait's economy opened the door to employment opportunities. With this, came a demand for labor that the native Kuwaiti was unable to meet, leaving the majority of jobs to be filled by expatriate labor.

(2) The young age of the Kuwaiti population. It is interesting to note that half of the Kuwaiti population is less than 15 years of age.

(3) The high illiteracy rate among the Kuwaiti labor force.

(4) The small part played by women in the Kuwaiti labor force. Though it is increasing steadily, Kuwaiti women's participation in the labor force remains small.

(5) The refusal of many to undertake any kind of manual work. Managerial, professional and government jobs are considered more prestigious.

The purpose of this book is to analyze the shortage of manpower in Kuwait and to propose solutions. In particular, we seek to examine four observations:

(1) Because of a unique combination of historical and social factors, Kuwait was unprepared for the impact of rapid growth.

(2) The lack of a comprehensive economic plan — one of the major factors contributing to manpower problems in Kuwait.

(3) Present massive educational programmes will not solve the manpower shortage.

(4) Instability in the Middle East has been beneficial for the supply of labor in Kuwait.

This will require the analysis of recent and current trends in the labor force, including growth of employment, immigration, structure of the labor force, distribution according to sector, occupation, educational level and nationality. The impact of these trends on Kuwaiti development prospects will be discussed.

xiv

Chapter 1 will begin with an analysis of the social, economic and political structure of Kuwait prior to the discovery of oil. This is essential for a proper understanding of the problem. Chapter 2 reveals the manpower structure in Kuwait and presents an analysis of the factors responsible for the very low participation rate of Kuwaitis in the labor force. Chapter 3 is devoted to a discussion of foreign manpower in Kuwait — one cannot discuss the Kuwaiti labor force without taking into account the non-Kuwaiti labor force, which constitutes 75 per cent of the total labor force in Kuwait. Chapter 4 looks at education and manpower in Kuwait and at government measures to deal with the manpower shortage through educational means. The final chapter is devoted to the development of a manpower plan for Kuwait.

# Chapter 1

# Pre-oil Kuwait

## Geography

Kuwait is a small Arab state located at the north-west corner of the Arabian Gulf. Bounded by Iraq to the north and Saudi Arabia to the west and south, it has an area of 17,280 sq. km, excluding the Neutral Zone, an area of mainly sand and desert with an off-shore area of nine islands.[1] Kuwait shares the Neutral Zone with Saudi Arabia and the area is administered jointly by the two countries. The natural resources of the zone are shared by the two countries.[2]

Kuwait has a natural bay extending 45 kilometers westward into the state. It was this natural bay, together with its geographical location, that helped Kuwait to become a major trade center in the Gulf area prior to the discovery of oil.

## People

The Arab population of Kuwait originates mainly from the Najd region of Arabia. The first tribe to settle in present-day Kuwait was the Beni Khalid, in 1688. It was followed by other tribes, among them the Utubi tribe, which is descended from the famous Arab tribe the Anaizz, originating from central Arabia. The ruling family of Kuwait – the Al Sabah family – and other merchant families in Kuwait belong to these tribes.[3]

Once Kuwait had become established as a major trade center in the Gulf area, Persian and Indian people began to settle there. The Persian community in Kuwait is in fact one of the oldest and, unlike the Arab majority, that follows the Suni sect of Islam, adheres to the Shia sect of Islam. Integration of the two communities in Kuwait continues to be

1

hindered by their respective clan and tribal attitudes. Intermarriage among the two communities is almost non-existent.[4]

Prior to 1948 there was a small Jewish community in Kuwait but this disappeared with the establishment of the State of Israel in that year.

Social stratification among the various tribes was predominant. The tribes that bred camels were considered the noblest, while the tribes that bred sheep and goats were considered to be of lower status;[5] farming and manual work were the least respected, and were actually deplored by the Bedouin Arabs.[6] The following story further illustrates this point:[7]

> About fifty years ago, the tale goes, Shaikh Mubarak Al Sabah, who was then the Amir, saw a Bedouin coming through one of the city gates leading a number of donkeys loaded with sacks of burned lime. The Shaikh approached the man, looked at him carefully, and said, 'Aren't you a member of the Ajman? ' The Ajman were among the most noble tribes in the country and a branch of the Sharif, who could trace their ancestors back for centuries.
>
> The Bedouin admitted that he was an Ajman, and the Shaikh said, 'You must know that an occupation such as burning lime shames a man of your quality.'
>
> 'My family and I had nothing to eat,' the Bedouin pleaded. 'We were near starvation. This was the only work I could find to support myself and my family.'
>
> But Shaikh Mubarak would accept no excuses. 'You have lowered yourself in the sight of God and your fellow tribesmen,' he said, 'I order you to abandon this unclean work immediately.'

Attitudes such as this have been modified somewhat but in general Kuwaitis still tend to look down on manual labor. This attitude can be traced to the Bedouin dislike of settled life, as perceived through the peasant who uses his hands. As Raphael Patai has put it:[8]

> One of the basic features of the Bedouin ethos is a contempt for all physical labor with the exception of tending of the livestock and raiding, which are considered the only fitting occupations for free men.

Although great economic changes have occurred in Kuwait during the post-war years, tribal and clan relationships continue to prevail. It is not uncommon to hear a young graduate speak proudly of his tribal ancestry. One can, furthermore, still witness the 'separation of tribes', in which it is considered taboo to intermarry into a tribe that does not meet your tribe's standards (i.e. belong to a well known Arab tribe).[9]

2

Tribal and family loyalties were reflected in the administration of Kuwait prior to its independence, when major posts were held by members of the ruling family and by other members of the merchant class.[10]

The merchant class attempted to reform the autocratic system of rule. Their limited success can be traced back to 1921 when they demanded from the new Amir, Shaikh Ahmed Al Jaber Al Sabah (1921-50), the formation of a Consultative Council. The merchants' demands were met and they elected twelve members, who were representatives of prominent Kuwaiti families. Unfortunately, the council was short lived as a result of internal disputes among its members. Thereafter, Kuwait continued to be run as it had been in the past.[11]

A second attempt at establishing a legislative assembly took place during 1937-8, when a fourteen-member council was selected from the merchant society and this council drafted a constitution calling for the election of a twenty-member council by the people.[12] Article 3 of the five-point document drafted by the council stated: 'All internal concession and lease monopolies as well as external agreements and treaties cannot be considered legal and binding unless approved by the elected legislative assembly.'[13]

There was disagreement between the Amir and the council, however, and it was dissolved as a consequence. Despite its short-lived history, however, the legislative assembly succeeded in establishing a government department, which is considered by some to be the beginning of the modern Kuwaiti administrative structure.[14]

## The economy

Kuwait's basic lack of resources (apart from oil) and its geographical location forced its population to depend heavily on the sea as the major source of livelihood and trade, pearl-diving and boat-building flourished in the Gulf area prior to the discovery of oil.

### Trade

The favorable geographical location of Kuwait helped the population to become amongst the foremost traders in the Gulf region. In 1831 Lorimer, a British employee of the Indian Civil Service who travelled in the Persian Gulf, put Kuwait's share in the Gulf trade at $500,000 in imports and $100,000 in exports.[15]

3

Around 1863 Kuwait's imports from India (mainly Bombay) were 2 lakhs rupees (200,000) in value, while its exports reached 4 lakhs (400,000) rupees in value. As the Acting Political Resident and Consul General in the Persian Gulf at the time, Lewis Pelly, reported:[16]

> Here is a clean, active town, with a broad and open main bazzar and numerous solid stone dwelling houses stretching along this strand, and containing some 20,000 inhabitants, attracting Arab and Persian Merchants from all quarters by the equity of its rule and by the freedom of its trade. It imports from Malabar and Bombay some two Lackhs of Rupee Value, principally in Longcloths, rice, coffee, planks and spices. It exports some 800 horses at an average value of 300 rupees each, 40,000 rupees worth in miscellanies or say approximatley nearly four lackhs of rupees worth of exports against two and a half Lackhs of imports.

Kuwaiti merchants would transport the cargo of other nations in the Gulf area to India and Africa. The business of trans-shipment flourished in Kuwait, whereby Kuwaiti merchants exported goods to neighboring countries, mainly Iraq and Saudi Arabia: during the period 1940-5, for instance, Iraq imported 17 per cent of its goods through Kuwait.[17] The re-trade with Saudi Arabia at the time was so substantial that the Saudi Arabian ruler asked the Kuwaiti merchants to collect taxes from the Saudi merchants and have the money repaid to him. The Kuwaiti merchants, however, refused to comply, stating that trade must be free and that they therefore did not have the right to tax other people. The Saudi Arabian ruler reacted by prohibiting Saudi merchants from trading with Kuwait.[18]

Besides its good harbor, Kuwait's low taxes — import duties were between 4 and 6 per cent — provided a further reason for its flourishing trade and trans-shipment. During the years 1938-9 public revenue totalled £60,000 and two-thirds of this amount came from import duties.[19] The government taxed the trans-shipment goods.

Although trade in Kuwait flourished prior to the discovery of oil, Kuwait remained basically a very poor country. The average personal income during the time was low and the unskilled laborer lived at subsistence level.[20]

## Pearl-diving

The single most important item for export prior to oil was the pearl. The majority of the Kuwaiti population was in one way or another involved in the business of pearl-diving. Unfortunately no accurate records were kept of the numbers involved but some historians have estimated the number at between 10,000 and 15,000.[21] Others believed the number of sailors and divers to have been around 30,000; in 1920, a Kuwaiti historian estimated numbers at about 25,000 men.[22]

Pearl-diving was a seasonal occupation lasting from May to September. It operated along the following lines:

1  The Naukhuda (captain of the ship) owned and operated the ship.
2  The divers were the laborers, who lived and searched for the oysters.
3  The Siyabs were those laborers responsible for letting the divers to the bottom of the sea, and who would pull them up when they had finished collecting the oysters.
4  The Radaifs were those laborers who helped the Siyabs in their jobs.

Before the beginning of the season the captain chose the crew. The divers would borrow money from the captain before the start of the season in order to support their families during their five-months absence. In so doing they had to agree to reimburse the captain and this system of credit, therefore, put them in debt before the start of the season even.

The divers received no salary for their work but shared the money from the sale of the pearls (provided they found some).[23] The profit was divided as follows:[24]

| | |
|---|---|
| Naukhuda: | one-fifth of the profit after expenses for food had been deducted (5 shares) |
| Divers: | 3 shares |
| Siyabs: | 2 shares |
| Radaifs: | 1 share |

In many instances, when the divers did not find any pearls, they were obliged to return the following season in order to repay the old season debt with the new season's added to it. If the divers suffered illness or death, a brother or son was obliged to replace him until the debt was repaid. J. R. Wellsted, who traveled in the Persian Gulf during the nineteenth century, described it thus:[25]

The following may be reckoned the common mode of proceeding: Five ghowass or divers and five siyabs or pullers up, agreed to take a boat together: the capitalist may probably already have lent these men about two hundred and fifty crowns to support their families during the former part of the year; perhaps they were unfortunate in the fishery of last years and gained little. It is supposed they may gain in the current year what the capitalist, in his generosity, may value and receive for one thousand german crowns, which is considered fair success, perhaps above the common. For a season the division would be as follows:

| | |
|---|---:|
| Total Value Acquired — German Crown | 1000 |
| Deduct final one eleventh of the Capital for the Boat | 90 |
| | 910 |
| Secondly, 250 Crowns advanced, generally in food and Clothing | 250 |
| | 660 |
| Thirdly, 100 percent on 250 Crowns advances | 250 |
| | 410 |
| Fourthly, 5 Crowns from each fisherman paid as tax to the Sheik or Chief of the Island | 50 |
| Balance | 360 |

to be divided among the ten fishermen, leaving thirty-six german crowns to each.

It should be mentioned here that the captain would borrow money from the pearl merchant (Tawash) in order to pay his workers. Eventually, the merchant took over the ship, and the captain and the workers began their work for him. The merchant's takeover put an end to the master tradesman concept, represented by the captain, and thus a new economic relationship emerged that was to have a profound impact on Kuwaiti society. It should be stressed, however, that the merchants continued to give the laborers shares instead of a paid salary. It was divided in the following manner:[26]

| | |
|---|---|
| The Naukhuda (captain) | 3 shares |
| The Ghowass (divers) | 3 shares |
| The Siyab (pull upman) | 2 shares |
| The Radaif (assistant to Siyab) | 1 share |

Pearl-diving was considered one of the most difficult and risky jobs, due mainly to the presence of sharks and sawfish in the Gulf waters. The divers worked from sunrise to sunset, only taking breaks to eat and pray. They spent all day going to the depths of the Gulf, collecting oysters and returning to the surface for breath, only to dive again. They lived on a diet of fish, dates and rice throughout the entire season. This poor diet certainly had a negative effect on their health, not to mention the hard work that went with it. As one traveler put it: 'Diving is considered very detrimental to health, and without doubt it shortens the life of those who much practice it.'[27] Others recorded: 'These men as might be expected, who pass one half of their lives in the most fatiguing of labors and the other half in dissipation, seldom live to an old age.'[28]

In spite of their harsh life, these men continued to work in the same tradition, for the sea was their only source of income. Kuwait's income from pearl trading was estimated to amount to 23 million rupees, or £1,688,888, annually.[29]

The 1930s, however, witnessed the industry's greatest setback, and ultimately its death-blow: the introduction of the Japanese cultured pearl. Kuwaiti merchants turned to an alternative source of income — smuggling, gold to India and goods to East Africa.[30]

**Boat-building**

Besides trade and pearl-diving, Kuwait became famous in the Gulf (prior to the discovery of oil) for boat-building. There were more than ten types of boat being made in Kuwait, and among them the Arab dhow became the best known.

The boats varied in size from the deep-sea dhow, called Baggala, used for the transportation of Iraqi dates to India and East Africa, to the smaller boat, called Belem, used in shallow water in the Gulf area, mainly for pearl-diving.[31]

In order to build a boat, the captain had to order his timber from India (in order to reduce the cost of the wood) and then contact a boat-builder, who in turn would hire the necessary carpenters, apprentices and coolies.

It is worth mentioning that the carpenter was usually paid only 2 or 3 rupees a day (one rupee was worth about 33 cents in 1937) and he worked from dawn to dusk; the coolies were lucky if they received one rupee.

The cost involved in boat-building depended greatly on the kind of wood used and on the size of the boat. Villiers put the cost of the boat that he traveled in during his journey in the Gulf during the years 1937-9 as follows:[32]

| | | |
|---|---|---|
| Cost of timber | Rupees | 6000 |
| Carpenter's contract price for labor | | 2800 |
| Sails | | 2000 |
| Masts | | 1000 |
| Longboat | | 200 |

7

Gear: including capstan, compass, binnacle, water tanks,
  firebox, four anchors and necessary roping stiffs and blocks
  caulking and paying stuffs including fish oil for inside
  and outside coats                                              100
Gig                                                               60
                                                             _____
TOTAL                                                        12,160

It is clear that the cost of a fairly large boat was relatively low and that the reason for this low cost can be attributed to the cheap labor and inexpensive wood used in building. By 1939 the rate of boat-building was two or three boats for deep water, with a proportional number for coastwise trade every month.[33] The precise number of people employed in boat-building remains unknown — however, one author has estimated the number to be around 300.[34]

It is interesting to note that the skilled laborers who built the boats came to Kuwait from Bahrain Island. They were Arabs but, because they belonged to the Shia sect of Islam, historians considered them to be of Persian origin, whilst other historians considered them to be Arabs who converted to the Shia sect of Islam. The boat-building skills were imported through the Bahraini immigrants, who had a long tradition in this particular trade.[35]

## Summary

Prior to the discovery of oil in 1938, Kuwaiti society resembled that of other basically traditional Arab countries. The tribal and extended family relationship was predominant and that relationship, by its very nature, prevented social integration among various groups. There was, for example, the widespread practice in Kuwaiti-Muslim marriages of marrying the uncle's daughter, or, as she is commonly called in Arabic, the Bint al Amm. The obvious reason for this practice can be explained in terms of an Arab's sentimentality to his kinsmen; though there is also to be seen an economic motive, in the desire to keep land and property within the kinship group. It can also be viewed as an attempt to avoid paying the full bride-wealth,[36] and a further explanation could be found in political motives since the father of the bride gained the support of his brother and his brother's son through such a practice.

Because the economy of Kuwait was simple and operated at a subsistence level, the manpower available in Kuwait was sufficient to perform the tasks for the economy at that time. There were large numbers of Persian and Negro (descendents of slaves) workers in the Kuwaiti

8

labor force of the time.[37] As mentioned, the skilled laborers who were employed in boat-building came mostly from the lower Gulf areas, mainly from Oman and Bahrain.

High-level manpower, (i.e. doctors, engineers, architects and teachers) was absent in Kuwait prior to the discovery of oil. Despite the fact that public education was institutionalized in Kuwait as early as 1912, it lacked the necessary high level of manpower, and education in public schools was limited to the teaching of Arabic, religion and mathematics.

The movement toward public education in Kuwait was initiated by the merchant class with the help and assistance of certain religious scholars (mostly Kuwaitis), amongst whom there were two Egyptians and one Tunisian scholar.[38] The first Kuwaiti university graduates began to trickle in during the late 1940s and early 1950s but because of their limited number the development of the country was a most difficult, if not impossible, task to accomplish without the help of a foreign labor force.

During the pre-oil era Kuwait was characterized by those features most common to underdeveloped countries: a very low per capita income, a low annual savings rate, an almost zero rate of growth, and seasonal unemployment.[39]

# Chapter 2

# Manpower in Kuwait

## Kuwait's economy after the discovery of oil

There is no doubt that the development of present-day Kuwait can be attributed largely to oil. Interest in Kuwait's oil was initiated as early as 1911, when a foreign oil company, the Anglo-Persian Oil Company (APOC), inquired of the British political resident in the Gulf Area whether it was possible to obtain an oil concession from the ruler of Kuwait. By 1914 APOC had sent a geological survey to Kuwait, and other oil companies were showing interest in Kuwait's oil.

In 1923 Major Holmes, of Eastern and General Syndicate (EGS), arrived in Kuwait and offered better terms than APOC for a concession. The ruler became interested in the Holmes offer, and Holmes then visited the USA in order to negotiate with major American oil companies. By 1928 Holmes had returned to Kuwait representing EGS and Gulf Oil Company.

The British Colonial Office became alarmed by the American oil company's presence in Kuwait and they warned the Kuwaiti ruler that any future oil concessions must include a British oil company, according to an earlier agreement between Kuwait and Great Britain. There was much negotiation between the various interests and finally the American government intervened on behalf of Gulf Oil in 1928. The dispute between the American oil company as represented by Gulf, and the Anglo-Persian oil company was resolved in 1934 through the formation of a joint company, to be called Kuwait Oil Company (KOC).[1]

Drilling by KOC was begun in 1934 but it was not until 1946 that the first commercial shipment of crude oil took place. As the production of oil increased rapidly so did Kuwait's revenue and by 1976 Kuwait's revenue from oil was estimated at around $7 billion.

It is difficult to classify Kuwait's economy as developed or under-developed, since Kuwait could be said to fall somewhere between. On the one hand, Kuwait is renowned for the highest per capita income in the world — in 1976 it was approximately $11,000 or KD 3,197.[2] The growth rate ranges between 8 and 10 per cent annually.[3] The country also enjoys a high rate of savings and a consistently favorable balance of payments. On the negative side, however, Kuwait resembles many of the less developed countries. It is totally reliant on a single resource — oil — which constitutes 98.1 per cent of total government revenue. It also suffers from a severe overdependence on imports because Kuwait produces very little besides oil, it imports almost everything (material goods, foods, etc.) from abroad (see table 2.1). Finally it suffers from an inadequate indigenous supply of labor and technically skilled workers.[4]

## Population and the labor force

### Population growth and composition

Official information on the population of Kuwait is lacking before the first census in 1957. It has been estimated, however, that before the discovery of oil in 1938 the population was 75,000.

After the discovery of oil the population growth-rate became one of the highest in the world, with an annual rate of increase of 9.8 per cent.[5] This high rate of increase is attributed to the influx of the foreign labor force. Kuwait's population doubled within ten years and tripled within twelve. Thus, the population in Kuwait increased almost five times within a twenty-year period (see table 2.2).

Table 2.2 shows that the annual rate of growth among the *total* population declined from 11.7 per cent during the years 1957–61 to 9.8 per cent during 1961–5, and to 6.1 per cent during the 1970–5 period.

The growth-rate among the Kuwaiti population, however, has fluctuated constantly. During the period 1957–61 it rose to 9.2 per cent and for the period 1961–5 it declined to 8 per cent, but it went up again in 1965–70, only to decline again to 6.4 per cent during 1970–5. This fluctuation can be attributed to naturalization and immigration.[6]

The growth-rate among the non-Kuwaiti population is higher than among the Kuwaiti population for the period 1957–70. Although it declined during 1975, the number of non-Kuwaiti still increased five times during the nine years 1957–65, and more than doubled, over the

**Table 2.1**   *Import figures and oil revenue, 1954–80 (KD million)*

| Year | Oil revenue | Imports |
|---|---|---|
| 1954 | 69.3 | 29.9 |
| 1955 | 100.5 | 32.9 |
| 1956 | 104.4 | 41.4 |
| 1957 | 110.2 | 55.6 |
| 1958 | 127.4 | 75.1 |
| 1959 | 167.0 | 93.2 |
| 1960 | 159.0 | 86.4 |
| 1961–2 | 167.0 | 89.0 |
| 1962–3 | 173.0 | 101.9 |
| 1963–4 | 190.6 | 115.7 |
| 1964–5 | 206.5 | 115.1 |
| 1965–6 | 225.5 | 134.7 |
| 1966–7 | 231.6 | 165.3 |
| 1967–8 | 263.0 | 211.9 |
| 1968–9 | 242.9 | 218.3 |
| 1969–70 | 280.6 | 230.7 |
| 1970–1 | 298.0 | 223.3 |
| 1971–2 | 354.1 | 232.3 |
| 1972–3 | 505.9 | 262.1 |
| 1973–4 | 543.9 | 310.6 |
| 1974–5 | 2,056.5 | 455.1 |
| 1975–6 | 1,703.4 | 693.2 |
| 1976–7 | 2,598,276 | 972.0 |
| 1977–8 | 2,575,361 | 1,387.0 |
| 1978–9 | 3,036,079 | 1,264.0 |
| 1979–80 |  | 5,940,458/NA |

Source: Ministry of Planning, Central Statistical Office, *Annual Statistical Abstract 1976*, pp. 184, 270; *Annual Statistical Abstract 1979*, p. 231, table 212, p. 298, table 251, 1980, pp. 241, 313, table 221, 265.

decade 1965–75. Their share of the total population rose from 45 per cent to 53 per cent during the period 1957–70. In 1975 their share of the total population declined to 52.5 per cent. However, the foreign population in Kuwait still constitutes a majority of the total population; and, more important, it also constitutes 75 per cent of Kuwait's labor force. (The foreign labor force in Kuwait will be discussed further in chapter 3.)

## Population by age

According to the UN Economic and Social Council the proportion of the population in the labor force in the Middle East is among the lowest in the world. This is attributed to the large number of children in the population.[7] In fact, with almost 50 per cent of the population under the age of 15 years, Kuwait can be considered to be among the 'youngest' countries in the world.[8] (See table 2.3.)

**Table 2.2** Population growth, by sex and major population group

| Year | Sex | Kuwaiti | | | Non-Kuwaiti | | | Total | | |
|---|---|---|---|---|---|---|---|---|---|---|
| | | No. | % of total population | Growth rate p.a. | No. | % of total population | Growth rate p.a. | Total population | % of total population | Growth rate p.a. |
| 1957 | Total | 113,622 | 55.0 | – | 92,851 | 45.0 | – | 206,473 | 100.0 | – |
| | Male | 59,154 | 28.6 | | 72,904 | 35.3 | | 132,058 | 63.9 | |
| | Female | 54,468 | 26.4 | | 19,947 | 9.7 | | 74,415 | 36.1 | |
| 1961 | Total | 161,909 | 50.4 | 9.2 | 159,712 | 49.6 | 14.5 | 321,621 | 100.0 | 11.7 |
| | Male | 84,461 | 26.3 | | 116,246 | 36.1 | | 200,707 | 62.4 | |
| | Female | 77,448 | 24.1 | | 43,466 | 13.5 | | 120,914 | 37.6 | |
| 1965 | Total | 220,059 | 47.1 | 8.0 | 247,280 | 52.9 | 11.5 | 467,339 | 100.0 | 9.8 |
| | Male | 112,569 | 24.1 | | 173,743 | 37.2 | | 286,312 | 61.3 | |
| | Female | 107,490 | 23.0 | | 73,537 | 15.7 | | 181,027 | 38.7 | |
| 1970 | Total | 347,396 | 47.0 | 9.6 | 391,266 | 53.0 | 9.6 | 738,662 | 100.0 | 9.6 |
| | Male | 175,513 | 23.7 | | 244,368 | 33.1 | | 419,881 | 56.8 | |
| | Female | 171,883 | 23.3 | | 146,898 | 19.9 | | 318,781 | 43.2 | |
| 1975 | Total | 472,088 | 47.5 | 6.4 | 522,749 | 52.5 | 5.9 | 994,837 | 100.0 | 6.1 |
| | Male | 236,600 | 23.8 | | 307,168 | 30.9 | | 543,768 | 54.7 | |
| | Female | 235,488 | 23.7 | | 215,581 | 21.6 | | 451,069 | 45.3 | |

Source: Industrial Bank of Kuwait, *Labor Force Statistics of Kuwait*, August 16, 1976.

**Table 2.3** *Distribution of population, by age-group, 1970 and 1975*

| Age-group | Kuwaiti | | | | | Non-Kuwaiti | | | | | Total | | | | |
|---|---|---|---|---|---|---|---|---|---|---|---|---|---|---|---|
| | *M* | *F* | *Total* | *% 1970* | *% 1975* | *M* | *F* | *Total* | *% 1970* | *% 1975* | *M* | *F* | *Total* | *% 1970* | *% 1975* |
| 0–14 | 118.1 | 115.4 | 233.5 | 49.4 | 50.1 | 106.0 | 101.4 | 207.4 | 39.7 | 37.1 | 224.1 | 216.8 | 440.9 | 44.3 | 43.2 |
| 15–19 | 23.5 | 25.4 | 48.9 | 10.4 | 10.0 | 21.3 | 16.4 | 37.7 | 7.2 | 6.8 | 44.8 | 41.8 | 86.6 | 8.7 | 8.3 |
| 20–34 | 48.9 | 52.7 | 101.6 | 21.5 | 20.7 | 95.0 | 59.6 | 154.6 | 29.6 | 35.6 | 143.9 | 112.3 | 256.2 | 25.8 | 28.6 |
| 35–54 | 33.9 | 29.5 | 62.5 | 13.2 | 13.3 | 76.7 | 32.2 | 108.9 | 20.8 | 18.1 | 109.7 | 61.7 | 171.4 | 17.2 | 15.8 |
| 55–64 | 7.4 | 7.0 | 14.4 | 3.1 | 2.8 | 6.3 | 3.4 | 9.7 | 1.9 | 1.5 | 13.7 | 10.4 | 24.1 | 2.4 | 2.1 |
| 65 and over | 5.7 | 5.5 | 11.2 | 2.4 | 2.8 | 1.9 | 2.5 | 4.4 | 0.8 | 0.7 | 7.6 | 8.0 | 15.6 | 1.6 | 1.7 |
| Total | 237.5 | 235.5 | 472.1 | 100.1 | 100.1 | 307.2 | 215.5 | 522.7 | 100.0 | 100.0 | 543.8 | 543.8 | 994.8 | 100.0 | 100.0 |

Source: Industrial Bank of Kuwait, *Labor Force Statistics of Kuwait*, August 1976 (memorandum).
Note: Total includes those whose age is not stated.

The young age of the Kuwaiti population makes dependence on a foreign labor force unavoidable. However, it should also mean that these young people in time will be able to replace the expatriate labor, or at least reduce their number. Needless to say, this will require proper preparation (education, training skills, etc.) according to the type of employment needed by the economy.

The population under 15 years of age, and which is not part of the labor force, can be considered a liability because it accounts for a large proportion of the social services expenditure (i.e., education, health and other services).[9] These services in turn require manpower, which the native population cannot provide.

The structure of the active population is unfavorable, in that there are about 50 inactive persons for every 50 active ones, as against a corresponding ratio of about 60 per cent for the developed countries.[10]

Table 2.3 shows that the percentage of non-Kuwaitis under 15 years of age is lower than that for Kuwaitis. In 1975 non-Kuwaitis accounted for only 37.1 per cent. This figure is explained by the fact that most of the immigrants who have come to Kuwait are of working age.

The number of males is higher than the number of females for both the Kuwaiti and non-Kuwaiti population.

There are various reasons for the large percentage of young people among the Kuwaiti population:

1 The natural birth-rate among the Kuwaiti population is very high–close to 4 per cent annually.[11] Early marriage among Kuwaitis contributes to this high birth-rate.[12]
2 Improved health facilities are keeping more children alive than ever before.
3 The rising affluence among Kuwaitis has meant that another child brings no financial problems, especially when the state pays for the health care and the education of children.

Kuwaitis outnumber non-Kuwaitis in all other population categories other than the labor force, which accounts for 30.6 per cent of the total population. Among the remaining 69.4 per cent of the population the following observations should be noted:

1 Children under 14 years of age account for 44.3 per cent of the total population. Of these, 52.9 per cent are Kuwaitis and 47.1 per cent are non-Kuwaitis.
2 Full-time students in 1976 numbered 201,907, i.e. 20.2 per cent of the total population. Of these, 121,244, or 60.1 per cent, were Kuwaiti and 80,663 (39.9 per cent) were non-Kuwaiti.

## The labor force in Kuwait

Generally manpower is defined as that part of the nation's population that is engaged in producing goods and services entering into the Gross National Product.[13] Manpower can also be defined as the 'active-age' persons available for work. Manpower in Kuwait is made up of those between the ages of 15 and 65 years who are available for work. According to the 1975 census they totalled 304,582 people, about 30.6 per cent of the total population. The number of males was 296,376 (88.4 per cent) and the number of females was 35,306 (11.6 per cent of the total manpower).

*Kuwaiti* manpower numbered only 91,844 persons, or 19.5 per cent of the total population. The number of non-Kuwaitis in the labor force was 212,738, or 40.7 per cent of the total non-Kuwaiti population.[14] (See table 2.4.)

As can be seen from table 2.4, the population of Kuwait has more than doubled during the ten years from 1965 to 1975. Nevertheless, the labor participation rate among Kuwaiti and non-Kuwaiti males declined during the same period, while the participation rate for both Kuwaiti and non-Kuwaiti females increased from 1 per cent to 3.2 per cent for Kuwaiti females, and from 10.4 per cent to 12.9 per cent for non-Kuwaiti females.

It is interesting to note that the participation rate for non-Kuwaiti women is four times higher than that for Kuwaiti women. The major obstacle against Kuwaiti women's full participation in the labor force is a social one: the traditional society in Kuwait limits women from participating completely in the economy. Even when a woman enters the labor force, she always takes a job that is considered by society to be 'proper' for a women (i.e., education, social work, nursing and medicine). Although there are no government restrictions against female participation in any job available, women in Kuwait continue to prefer to work in these traditional jobs because of the stigma that would attach to them if they did otherwise.

It should be stressed here that even though the law does not specifically prohibit women from accepting any job, it is, however, customary to prohibit a woman from becoming a judge or from holding any number of positions in the diplomatic service.

The most obvious discrimination against women is in their political rights. Although Article 29 of the Kuwait Constitution states: 'All people are equal in human dignity, and in public rights and duties before the law, without distinction as to race, origin, language or religion. . .'[15] we find that women are discriminated against by law.

**Table 2.4** *Labor force, by nationality and participation rate*

| Year | Kuwaiti | | | Non-Kuwaiti | | | Total population | | |
|---|---|---|---|---|---|---|---|---|---|
| | *M* | *F* | *Total* | *M* | *F* | *Total* | *M* | *F* | *Total* |
| *1965* | | | | | | | | | |
| Population (000) | 112.5 | 107.5 | 222.1 | 173.7 | 73.5 | 247.2 | 286.3 | 181.0 | 467.3 |
| Labor force (000) | 41.9 | 1.1 | 43.0 | 133.6 | 7.7 | 141.3 | 175.5 | 8.8 | 184.3 |
| Participation rate (%) | 37.2 | 1.0 | 19.5 | 76.9 | 10.4 | 57.1 | 61.3 | 4.8 | 39.4 |
| *1970* | | | | | | | | | |
| Population | 175.5 | 171.9 | 347.4 | 244.4 | 146.9 | 391.3 | 419.8 | 318.8 | 738.6 |
| Labor force | 63.3 | 2.0 | 65.3 | 162.3 | 14.5 | 176.8 | 225.6 | 16.6 | 242.2 |
| Participation rate (%) | 36.1 | 1.2 | 18.8 | 66.4 | 9.9 | 45.2 | 53.7 | 5.2 | 32.8 |
| *1975* | | | | | | | | | |
| Population | 236.6 | 235.5 | 472.1 | 307.1 | 215.6 | 522.7 | 543.7 | 451.1 | 994.8 |
| Labor force | 84.3 | 7.5 | 91.8 | 185.0 | 27.7 | 212.7 | 269.4 | 35.2 | 304.6 |
| Participation rate (%) | 35.7 | 3.2 | 19.5 | 60.3 | 12.9 | 40.7 | 49.5 | 7.8 | 30.6 |

Source. Industrial Bank of Kuwait, *Labor Force Statistics of Kuwait*, August 1976 (memorandum).

For instance, in Qanon No. 35, for the year 1963 (a law relating to the elections for the National Assembly), women are excluded from the right to vote as citizens, unlike their male counterparts. The right to vote and run for public office is only given to males over 21 years of age.

Discrimination against women exists in other aspects of the law, such as nationality. The law states that, if a Kuwaiti male marries a foreigner, his wife will be a Kuwaiti citizen after a period from 1 to 5 years. On the other hand, if a Kuwaiti woman marries a foreigner, she normally loses her Kuwaiti nationality.[16] Discrimination against women by law is here more than obvious. It does not seem logical that Kuwaiti women are not given the same rights as men, especially since it is well known that Kuwait is faced by a severe shortage of manpower: it would therefore seem in the national interest to give nationality to a man who married a Kuwaiti woman. In Kuwait, however, as with the rest of the Arab countries, a woman's nationality follows that of her husband.

The low participation of Kuwaiti women in the labor force is one of the major causes of the manpower shortage in Kuwait.

## Distribution of the labor force according to economic sector

Because the labor force is a major element of social and economic development, it is essential to look at the structure and distribution of labor force, since it indicates the level and the stage of development in the country.

The highest proportion of the labor force is concentrated in services which include government as well as personal services and banking.[17] This sector employs 55.8 per cent of the total labor force (table 2.5).

Table 2.5 shows that there is a general imbalance in the distribution of the labor force, which is indicative of the high dependence on the government as a major employer. The failure of other sectors in the economy to create employment opportunities rapidly enough to absorb the increase in the labor force also contributes to this imbalance in the distribution of the labor force.

It is worth mentioning here that Kuwait does not differ much from the other less developed countries where the government is the largest single employer. Some African countries are an example of this: for example, employment in the government sector in Ghana, Kenya, Nigeria, Tanzania and Uganda is significantly high.[18]

**Table 2.5** *Labor force, by economic sector, 1975*

| | Kuwaiti | % | non-Kuwaiti | % | Total | % |
|---|---|---|---|---|---|---|
| Agriculture, forestry & hunting | 3,983 | 4.6 | 3,531 | 1.7 | 7,514 | 2.6 |
| Mining & quarrying | 1,779 | 2.0 | 3,080 | 1.5 | 4,859 | 1.6 |
| Manufacturing | 2,258 | 2.6 | 22,209 | 10.5 | 24,467 | 8.2 |
| Construction | 1,756 | 2.0 | 30,500 | 14.4 | 32,256 | 10.8 |
| Electricity, gas & water | 2,034 | 2.3 | 5,237 | 2.5 | 7,271 | 2.4 |
| Commerce | 6,327 | 7.3 | 33,232 | 15.7 | 39,559 | 13.3 |
| Transport, storage & commerce | 4,567 | 5.3 | 11,118 | 5.2 | 15,685 | 5.3 |
| Services | 64,265 | 73.9 | 102,537 | 48.5 | 166,802 | 55.8 |
| Activities not adequately stated | 2 | – | – | – | – | – |

Source: Industrial Bank of Kuwait, *Labor Force Statistics of Kuwait*, August 1976 (memorandum).

The question that arises here is: Why is the majority of the labor force concentrated in the government sector? The answer lies in the government welfare system and its employment policy. The government welfare system which guarantees every inhabitant of Kuwait a free education, free health and other services, has led to the expansion of government services and has thereby created new job opportunities, which have been filled by the expatriate labor force because the native population has been unable to provide the necessary manpower.

Government employment policy is designed to promote a more equitable distribution of income among the Kuwait population. Thus a policy of guaranteed employment for every Kuwaiti citizen has been adopted. As stated in Article 41 of the Constitution:[19]

Every Kuwaiti has the right to work and to choose the type of his work. Work is a duty of every citizen necessitated by personal dignity and public good. The State shall endeavour to make it available to citizens and to make its terms equitable.

A comparison between Kuwaitis and non-Kuwaitis shows that the second highest concentration of labor is in commerce, where Kuwaitis number 6,327 as opposed to more than five times that number for non-Kuwaiti employees. In spite of the high percentage of non-Kuwaitis in

19

this sector, ownership of business is granted only to Kuwaiti citizens. (This will be discussed further in chapter 3.)

For non-Kuwaitis the third highest concentration of labor is in construction, while for Kuwaiti labor it is in the field of transport, storage and communication. The low percentage of Kuwaitis in the construction field is explained by the fact that the Kuwaiti tends to refuse the type of employment which calls for manual labor. The Kuwaiti prefers to be employed as guardsman or communication supervisor rather than as a construction worker.

Fourth highest concentration of non-Kuwaiti workers is in the manufacturing sector, where there is a very low percentage of Kuwaiti employees (2.6 per cent of the total labor force).

Despite the fact that the oil industry is the backbone of Kuwait's economy and the only source of its wealth, the numbers employed in this field remain extremely low. The oil sector represented by the mining and quarrying occupations accounts for only 2 per cent of the total Kuwaiti labor force. In 1971 there were 7,140 employees, of whom 1,810 were of Kuwaiti nationality.

The original oil concession between the government of Kuwait and the oil companies included a clause giving priority in employment to the local labor force, followed by the non-Kuwaiti Arab labor force. As stated in Kuwait's Oil Concession Article 8, Clause B:[20]

> The Company shall employ subjects of the Shaikh as far as possible
> for all work for which they are suited under the supervision of the
> company's skilled employees, but if the local supply of labor should
> in the judgment of the company be inadequate or unsuitable the
> company shall have the right with the approval of the Shaikh which
> shall not be unreasonably withheld to import labor preference
> being given to laborers from the neighboring Arab countries who
> will obey the local laws.

In practice, however, the percentage of the native labor force has always been low.

It was only after independence in 1961, that the percentage of Arab and Kuwaiti employees surpassed the foreign labor force. Since this is a clear violation of the original terms in the Concession, one might raise the question here as to why the oil companies employed such a small percentage of the native labor force? One answer has been given by Joe Stark:[21]

> One reason for the relatively low employment was the industry's
> decision to construct refinery plants in the capitalist consuming

countries. Refinery operations use 3.5 times as many workers per ton of crude oil processed as simple crude extraction. As late as the mid-fifties total Petroleum Industry employment in the Middle East was 140,000 compared with textile factory employment in Egypt alone of 114,000.

A second reason for the limited employment in the oil industry is political. Many oil companies feared that if they trained the native labor to operate everything they would be taken over. This fear was well expressed in these words:[22]

Some Western oil men feel there is a limit beyond which no company can go in relinquishing operational control to local employees. Since a national of the Middle Eastern country may find difficulty in being completely loyal to his employer in a dispute with his own country, they maintain the only safe course is to limit local responsibility to a level compatible with the company's own security.

The argument of the oil companies was that there were not enough laborers to handle the sophisticated jobs. (See chapter 4 for a more detailed discussion.)

## Distribution of the labor force according to major occupational group

A study of the distribution of the labor force by major occupational group is essential for an understanding of the major manpower requirements for Kuwait, and for an awareness of the shortage (or over-employment) in the various occupational groups.

The distribution of the labor force by major occupational group indicates that Kuwaitis are outnumbered in every occupation. It also reveals that the majority of the labor force is concentrated in a relatively small occupational sector (see table 2.6).

Table 2.6 shows that while the number of Kuwaitis has increased considerably in every occupation since 1970, Kuwaitis remain a minority in every occupational group. The number of Kuwaitis in scientific and professional occupations has increased 2.5 times in five years. This can be attributed to the great emphasis on education, but it nevertheless remains a fact that Kuwaitis still account for less than the non-Kuwaitis in this occupational group.

The number of Kuwaitis in administrative and managerial jobs almost doubled during the five years 1970-5, the result of the

**Table 2.6** *Labor force, by major occupational group, 1970, 1975*

| Occupation | 1970 | | | | | | 1975 | | | | | |
| --- | --- | --- | --- | --- | --- | --- | --- | --- | --- | --- | --- | --- |
| | Kuwaiti | % | non-Kuwaiti | % | Total | % | Kuwaiti | % | non-Kuwaiti | % | Total | % |
| Scientific & professional | 3,734 | 6.1 | 21,888 | 12.4 | 25,622 | 10.8 | 9,739 | 11.2 | 32,097 | 15.2 | 41,836 | 14.0 |
| Administrative & managerial | 611 | 1.0 | 1,169 | 0.7 | 1,780 | 1.0 | 1,045 | 1.2 | 1,809 | 0.8 | 2,854 | 1.0 |
| Executive & clerical | 11,474 | 18.6 | 16,730 | 9.5 | 28,204 | 11.9 | 17,853 | 20.5 | 20,165 | 9.5 | 38,018 | 12.7 |
| Sales | 6,548 | 10.6 | 14,545 | 8.3 | 21,093 | 8.9 | 6,185 | 7.1 | 17,908 | 8.5 | 24,093 | 8.1 |
| Services | 23,216 | 37.6 | 34,521 | 19.6 | 57,737 | 24.3 | 32,900 | 37.8 | 45,400 | 21.5 | 78,300 | 26.2 |
| Agricultural & fisheries | 893 | 1.4 | 3,050 | 1.7 | 3,943 | 1.6 | 3,897 | 4.5 | 3,805 | 1.8 | 7,702 | 2.6 |
| Production and raw labor | 13,385 | 21.7 | 83,581 | 47.5 | 96,966 | 40.8 | 15,348 | 17.7 | 90,260 | 42.7 | 105,608 | 35.4 |
| Unclassified | 1,821 | 3.0 | 589 | 0.3 | 2,410 | 1.0 | 4 | – | – | – | 4 | – |
| Total | 61,682 | 100.0 | 176,073 | 100.0 | 237,755 | 100.3 | 86,971 | 100.0 | 211,444 | 100.0 | 298,415 | 100.0 |

Source: Industrial Bank of Kuwait, *Labor Force Statistics of Kuwait*, August 1976 (memorandum).

government's policy of 'Kuwaitization': the replacement of non-Kuwaitis with available and qualified Kuwaitis.

Of particular interest are the figures for the service sector: while the number of Kuwaitis increased by 9,684, the number of non-Kuwaitis increased by 10,879. This was during the time of the government's policy of Kuwaitization in the government sector. One explanation for the increased number of *non*-Kuwaitis in the government sector is an increased demand and need for teachers, doctors and engineers in the service sector.

In Table 2.7, the groups have been separated into selected scientific and professional groups of occupations, and the picture becomes

**Table 2.7**  *Selected professional and scientific occupations, by sex and nationality, 1975*

| Occupation | Total | Kuwaiti | non-Kuwaiti | % Kuwaiti |
|---|---|---|---|---|
| Teachers | 18,370 | 5,262 | 13,108 | 28.6 |
| m | 8,885 | 2,210 | 6,675 | 24.8 |
| f | 9,485 | 3,052 | 6,433 | 32.2 |
| Accountants | 3,562 | 249 | 3,313 | 6.9 |
| m | 3,371 | 207 | 3,164 | 6.1 |
| f | 191 | 42 | 149 | 21.9 |
| Engineers | 3,464 | 328 | 3,136 | 9.5 |
| m | 3,431 | 317 | 3,114 | 9.2 |
| f | 33 | 11 | 22 | 33.3 |
| Doctors | 1,764 | 225 | 1,539 | 12.7 |
| m | 1,489 | 183 | 1,306 | 12.2 |
| f | 275 | 42 | 233 | 15.2 |
| Economists | 164 | 58 | 106 | 35.4 |
| m | 130 | 32 | 98 | 24.6 |
| f | 34 | 26 | 8 | 76.5 |
| Lawyers | 797 | 267 | 530 | 33.5 |
| m | 764 | 242 | 522 | 31.7 |
| f | 33 | 25 | 8 | 75.8 |

Source: Ministry of Planning, Bureau of Census, *The Population Census 1975*, Government Printing, Kuwait, 2 vols, table 50.

clearer. This table again shows that Kuwaitis are outnumbered in every occupation — except for Kuwaiti female economists and lawyers, who outnumber their foreign counterparts. The reason for the higher number of Kuwaiti female lawyers is the Kuwaiti law that restricts non-Kuwaitis working as lawyers, forbidding them to defend a client without special permission from the Minister of Justice.

It should be noted that table 2.7 deals with people employed in the fields of economics, teaching, medicine, etc. It does not mention, however, the availability of employable graduates in these fields. For instance, the number of Kuwaitis graduating from Kuwait University alone, up until the year 1975, in the field of economics and political science was 165, and the number graduating in law was 141.[23] One can question here why only 58 Kuwaiti economists appeared in the government statistics as economists? One explanation for such a discrepancy can be found in 'disguised employment,' whereby people are employed in jobs not in keeping with their qualifications and experience.[24]

Many young Kuwaiti graduates choose to be employed by the government not because of their qualifications, or according to the needs of the job market, but rather because of their own personal preferences and the greater chance of promotion than in other sectors of the economy. The smaller the particular ministry institution, the better are the chances of being promoted more quickly; and these chances are further enhanced by the government's policy of Kuwaitization in the government sector.

Thus in Kuwait, like in the rest of the less developed countries, young graduates end up working in clerical jobs that could actually be performed by employees with a secondary or primary school certificate.[25] Numerous qualified Kuwaitis employed in the Kuwaiti labor force are therefore under-utilized (see chapter 5). In most less developed countries the problem of disguised employment and under-utilization of the labor force is associated with a lack of available jobs and an abundant labor supply.[26]

Despite the fact that Kuwait has a critical need for teachers, many Kuwaitis refuse to take jobs as teachers.[27] The main reasons for this are: (1) the availability of jobs in other government ministries – Harbison states that teachers in less developed countries are always in short supply because of the availability of other government jobs;[28] (2) the ministry of Education in Kuwait is the largest in the state, and the chance of promotion is thus very slight; (3) teaching jobs are considered hard work, requiring preparation and study; (4) the abundant supply of teachers from other Arab states has made it possible for Kuwaitis to look for employment in other fields.

The Kuwaiti government, in an effort to overcome the shortage of Kuwaiti teachers, initiated a program of providing teachers with a 'bonus salary,' referred to as 'Tabeeat Ameel,' meaning the nature of the job. This bonus salary is a 25 per cent increase on the basic salary. Another government incentive has been the appointment of Kuwaitis in high administrative jobs (see table 2.8).

**Table 2.8**   *Ministry of Education administrative staff, 1977-8*

| Occupation | Kuwaiti | non-Kuwaiti | Total | % Kuwaiti |
|---|---|---|---|---|
| Directors | 27 | 3 | 30 | 90 |
| Controllers | 46 | 7 | 53 | 87 |
| Asst controllers | 3 | 1 | 4 | 75 |
| Section heads | 80 | 42 | 122 | 66 |
| Branch heads | 55 | 83 | 138 | 40 |
| Inspectors | 24 | 288 | 312 | 8 |
| Experts and counsellors | – | 3 | 3 | 0 |
| Administrators | 692 | 1,688 | 2,380 | 29 |
| Attendants | 86 | 708 | 794 | 11 |
| Laborers | 428 | 1,355 | 1,783 | 24 |
| Watchmen | 107 | 51 | 158 | 68 |
| Total | 1,548 | 4,229 | 5,777 | 27 |

Source: Ministry of Education, Annual Report 1977-8.

A further examination of occupational groups below the scientific and professional occupations shows Kuwait to be extremely dependent on the foreign labor force. Table 2.9 shows that, with the exception of clerical jobs, the percentage of Kuwaitis employed is quite high. Here again, the question of developing Kuwait without foreign assistance is raised. The International Labor Office study of a number of Arab countries, including Kuwait, concluded:[29]

> Manpower projections indicate that foreign manpower will continue to be needed to sustain further growth and will increase at a rate more or less equivalent to that of Kuwaiti manpower. Lower increases in foreign manpower can only be achieved at the expense of economic growth.

Harbison and Myers argue that:[30]

> The underdeveloped countries are those whose economic and social progress is dependent upon continued employment of foreign high level manpower in a wide variety of core positions in major public and private institutions.

Kuwait can be said to fit the above classification because of her heavy dependence on foreign labor for her future economic development.

**Table 2.9**   *Technicians, skilled and semi-skilled workers, 1975*

|  | Kuwaiti | non-Kuwaiti | Total | % Kuwaiti |
|---|---|---|---|---|
| *Technicians* | | | | |
| Tech. assistants to physical & life scientists | 115 | 543 | 658 | 17.5 |
| Engin. Surveyors, draughts- men and related Tech. | 775 | 2,242 | 3,017 | 25.7 |
| Pharmacist Assist. | 97 | 251 | 348 | 28.0 |
| Nurses and Obstetricians | 64 | 2,007 | 2,071 | 3.1 |
| Total scientific and technical | 1,051 | 5,043 | 6,094 | 17.2 |
| Stenographers, typists & rel. | 1,266 | 4,298 | 5,564 | 22.7 |
| Bookkeepers, cashiers and rel. | 1,942 | 4,671 | 6,613 | 29.4 |
| Other clerical | 12,127 | 10,722 | 22,849 | 53.0 |
| Total clerical | 15,335 | 19,691 | 35,026 | 43.8 |
| Total techn. group | 16,386 | 24,734 | 41,120 | 39.8 |
| *Skilled & semi-skilled* | | | | |
| Prod. Supervisors & Foremen | 3,102 | 4,523 | 7,625 | 40.7 |
| Miners & Quarrymen, etc. | 78 | 218 | 296 | 26.3 |
| Chemical workers & Refiners | 274 | 500 | 774 | 35.4 |
| Carpenters | 194 | 2,987 | 3,181 | 6.1 |
| Blacksmiths | 164 | 1,538 | 1,702 | 9.6 |
| Assembly and Main- tenance Tech. | 1,741 | 8,487 | 10,228 | 17.0 |
| Electricians | 1,331 | 7,378 | 8,709 | 15.3 |
| Plumbers & Welders | 554 | 5,811 | 6,365 | 8.7 |
| Printing Workers | 390 | 690 | 1,080 | 36.1 |
| Total | 7,828 | 32,132 | 39,960 | 19.6 |

Source: Government of Kuwait, Ministry of Planning, *The Five-Year Development Plan 1977-1981.*

## Distribution of the labor force according to educational attainment

A study of the labor force according to educational attainment is essential for a proper understanding and evaluation of human-resources development in Kuwait. It will furthermore be helpful in assessing the manpower stock available.

Besides the small size and the young age of the native population, one of the major reasons for Kuwait's dependence on the foreign labor force is the low level of educational attainment amongst the Kuwaiti labor force. The proportion of Kuwaiti illiterates in the labor force is 35.9 per cent and if we add to this figure that of the semi-illiterate labor force (those people who read and write below the primary level), the figure rises to 59.3 per cent. This means that more than half the Kuwaiti labor force is illiterate. Some 14.2 per cent of the Kuwaiti labor force hold primary-school degrees, 11.9 per cent hold intermediate and 10.6 per cent hold certificates below university level (table 2.10).

Table 2.10 shows that Kuwait has a critical shortage of high-level manpower. This is further illustrated by the number of expatriates with university degrees – 20,962 as against only 3,488 Kuwaitis. Thus the number of expatriates holding a university degree is five times that for the native population.

Table 2.10 also shows that the bulk of both the native and the expatriate labor force has no formal education and that they form 58.7 per cent. In other words, only 41.3 per cent of the labor force has had a formal education. This contributes to low productivity in the government sector (see chapter 5).

The high illiteracy rate in Kuwait is indicative of the fact that investment in human capital has been moderate.[31]

Kuwait, without any doubt, has been able to benefit greatly from the 'brain drain' of other Arab and non-Arab Third World countries. Undoubtedly, this high-level foreign manpower has cost their respective governments great amounts of money in terms of education; Kuwait has been able to benefit from the education and skill.[32]

It is interesting to note that the educational level of both the Kuwaiti and non-Kuwaiti female labor force is higher than that of the males. A very high percentage of Kuwaiti females have completed primary, inter-mediate and secondary-school level. It goes without saying that if the social barriers against women's full participation could be removed, Kuwaiti women could fill many of the job areas in which there is presently a shortage of Kuwaiti manpower.

**Table 2.10** *Distribution of labor force according to educational attainment*

| | 1965 | | | | 1970 | | | | 1975 | | | |
|---|---|---|---|---|---|---|---|---|---|---|---|---|
| | *Kuwaiti* | *%* | *non-Kuwaiti* | *%* | *Kuwaiti* | *%* | *non-Kuwaiti* | *%* | *Kuwaiti* | *%* | *non-Kuwaiti* | *%* |
| Illiterate | 78,319 | 43.0 | 28,255 | 43.2 | 62,025 | 35.1 | 90,280 | 37.3 | 31,181 | 35.9 | 69,640 | 32.9 |
| Reads and writes | 72,462 | 39.3 | 21,391 | 32.8 | 56,344 | 31.8 | 77,735 | 32.1 | 20,398 | 23.4 | 53,705 | 25.4 |
| Elementary | 6,863 | 3.7 | 6,740 | 10.3 | 13,182 | 7.5 | 19,922 | 8.2 | 12,362 | 14.2 | 20,209 | 9.6 |
| Intermediate | 6,596 | 3.6 | 4,275 | 6.5 | 10,592 | 6.0 | 14,867 | 5.1 | 10,340 | 11.9 | 17,067 | 8.1 |
| Secondary & post-sec. | 12,778 | 7.5 | 3,449 | 5.3 | 22,313 | 12.6 | 25,762 | 10.6 | 9,199 | 10.6 | 29,861 | 14.0 |
| University & postgraduate | 5,297 | 2.9 | 1,219 | 1.9 | 12,016 | 6.8 | 13,235 | 5.5 | 3,488 | 4.0 | 20,962 | 10.0 |
| Unclassified | 100 | 0.0 | 40 | 0.0 | 355 | 0.2 | 395 | 0.2 | 3 | 0.0 | – | – |
| Total | 182,415 | 100.0 | 65,369 | 100.0 | 176,827 | 100.0 | 242,196 | 100.0 | 86,971 | 100.0 | 211,444 | 100.0 |

Source: Industrial Bank of Kuwait, *Labor Force Statistics of Kuwait*, August 1976 (memorandum).

## Summary

The point that has continuously been reiterated throughout this chapter is Kuwait's dependence on an expatriate labor force. Expatriate labor not only outnumbers native labor in all but one sector of the economy: it also outnumbers Kuwaiti labor in level of occupational and educational attainment.

The main cause for this heavy dependence on a foreign labor force is the sudden wealth that has come to Kuwait through the discovery of oil. The resultant rapid growth of the Kuwaiti economy has been the major contributing force to the severe manpower shortage, opening the door for jobs and opportunities for employment. Along with these job opportunities has come a high demand for labor which the native population for various reasons, has not been able to fulfill.

The manpower shortage in Kuwait is twofold: on one hand there is a shortage of native labor due to the young age of the Kuwaiti population, the low participation of women and the low educational attainment of the labor population. On the other hand, the productivity of the available labor force, especially in the government, is very low.

Again, we must question here the feasibility of developing a country in which the majority of its population is either civil servants or merchants.

The problem becomes even more acute when one becomes aware of the distribution of the labor force by occupational group. The percentage of Kuwaitis in the professional, technical and semi-technical fields is very low: for example, the proportion of Kuwaiti plumbers is 8.7 per cent, carpenters 6.1 per cent and blacksmiths 9.6 per cent. It can be stated here that if similar trends continue, Kuwait will be likely to experience a major manpower crisis in the event that the expatriate labor force, for one reason or another, decides to leave, or if it were forced to leave the country within a short period of time.

The fact that Kuwait has the highest birth-rate along with the most rapidly expanding population in the world, in which the rate of increase is 9 per cent annually, has been less than beneficial. On the contrary, one can say that this has probably increased the manpower shortage.

As mentioned earlier, those under 14 years of age constitute 50 per cent of the total population. Needless to say, this young segment of the population adds to the general need for services in the fields of education, health and social services.

It is fair to state that the high standard of living presently enjoyed in Kuwait is maintained mainly through the help and assistance of the expatriate labor force. The high-level manpower skills of the expatriate labor have helped Kuwait in its task of economic development, and continue to do so. These workers have helped transform Kuwait from a simple traditional society to a more modern transitional one.

If Kuwait had had to depend on its own manpower, it would have taken at least twenty years more to reach the state of development it has already achieved.[33]

Chapter 3 will address itself to a question that is becoming central to the continuous viability and prosperity of Kuwait: the presence of the foreign labor force in Kuwait, which accounts for more than 52 per cent of the total population.

# Chapter 3

# Foreign manpower

In the previous chapters, I indicated that Kuwait suffers from severe structural labor shortages. These shortages primarily began during Kuwait's post-oil era when the economy expanded rapidly but the country's population was small, young, and illiterate, thus necessitating assistance from a foreign labor force.

The focus of this chapter will be foreign manpower in Kuwait, with particular emphasis being given to a discussion of the 'push' and 'pull' factors which facilitate migration. This will require an analysis of both the nature and flow of the phenomenon, and the development of a social, occupational and demographic profile of the migrants. An evaluation of the legal status of the foreign labor force will also be made.

## The pull factor

The principal pull factor for the foreign labor force in Kuwait is an economic one, the initial decision to emigrate to Kuwait, as well as the decision to stay in the host country, being largely determined by wage factors.[1] The 'wage differential' between the country of origin and Kuwait is generally very high, Kuwait ranking higher on the salary scale than most countries in the Middle East, including the other oil-producing states. This is evidenced by the presence of 45,070 people from Iraq, 49,482 from Iran, 12,527 from Saudi Arabia, and more than 14,000 from other Gulf states and Oman.[2] It may be noted that the majority of these employees are recent immigrants who have decided to settle in Kuwait.

Another pull factor has been the simple and easy migration policy. After the discovery of oil in Kuwait, an 'open-door' policy toward immigrant labor was adopted, under which any person willing to work was allowed into Kuwait. Such a policy was adopted to encourage and facilitate migration because of the rapid expansion taking place within Kuwait. However, it proved detrimental. This policy, unfortunately, adversely affected the native Kuwaiti labor, which began to find itself unemployed and without the necessary skills, and thus unable to compete with the foreign labor in the market. This led to widespread protest from the Kuwaitis and in 1954 the government established the 'Labor Office' with the purpose and intent of protecting the native labor force.

In early 1955 the Labor Office was expanded and the Ministry of Social Affairs and Labor was created. This ministry's first task was to register all the workers in Kuwait and to issue work-permit cards to them. To qualify for a work-permit card, the ministry required the person to: (1) have a passport; (2) enter the country legally (because many foreign workers, especially from Iran, Iraq and Saudi Arabia, enter the country illegally and refuse to register for fear of deportation).

The number of foreign manual workers in 1955 totalled 34,256; of these, 21,000 had entered the country illegally. This means that a substantial 61.3 per cent, i.e. the majority of these people, had entered the country illegally.[3] In 1961 the number of foreign workers surpassed that of the native labor force, causing the government to increase its restrictions on the entry of foreign labor. At present, employment of foreign labor in Kuwait is limited to the sectors in which there are no Kuwaitis available to fill the positions vacant. Despite such employment restrictions, the number of foreigners continues to increase annually, and the percentage of Kuwaitis in 1980 was only 41.5 per cent of the total population. Government restrictions on the entry of foreign labor, however, should benefit those foreign workers already in Kuwait, since the demand for their services should thereby increase, which should eventually close the gap in wages between them and their Kuwaiti counterparts.

Another significant pull factor is the availability of low-priced consumer goods, since there is no tax in Kuwait. This has attracted many people from socialist-orientated economies such as Iraq, Egypt, Syria, South Yemen and India to seek employment in Kuwait where they can buy low-priced consumer goods and send or take them home. Kuwait also provides free health services and schooling to every resident in the country, and has attracted many foreigners wishing to take advantage of such facilities.[4] Such obligations have been of concern to the government because of the increasing numbers of foreign workers, though they have of course needed the foreign labor and the merchants are naturally reluctant to disrupt the supply of cheap labor. The large foreign labor force in Kuwait of course leads to a stronger economy, not only because of their productivity but also because of their consumption.[5]

Compared with the rest of the Arab world, Kuwait, next to Lebanon, has a relatively high level of freedom of speech and press. Consequently, many professional Arabs have sought employment in Kuwait instead of other Arab Gulf states. Another important pull factor has been the general tolerance by Kuwaiti society of diverse and substantial numbers of foreigners. As indicated in chapter 1, prior to the discovery of oil the Kuwait merchants traveled in the Gulf, Africa, and India; this contact with other people has contributed to making the Kuwaitis more liberal in their attitude toward others. It is not totally by accident that many Arabs, Iranians, Pakistanis and Indians prefer to work in Kuwait and not in other oil-producing states in the Gulf.

## The push factor

Most studies concerning foreign labor migration to Kuwait have emphasized economics as the major cause. Thus, little attention has been given to such non-economic factors as the social and political attractions.

One of the major push factors to Kuwait is the high employment and under-employment in the countries neighboring Kuwait – primarily Iraq, Iran, Oman and Yemen. One of the causes of unemployment in less developed countries is the migration of peasants from the country-side to the cities, seeking jobs.[6] This migration evolved as a result of the low rate of return for labor in the agricultural sector along with continuous under-employment and seasonal unemployment. (In Iraq, for example, seasonal unemployment reached 75–80 per cent in the agricultural sector.[7]) Thus, many young people who had worked in agriculture migrated to the cities for better job opportunities. They quickly discovered, however, that no jobs were available. The only option left open to them was (and still is) to migrate to other countries, particularly the oil-producing states where jobs exist. Kuwait, like Saudi Arabia, Bahrain, and the United Arab Emirates, has its share of the Persian, Iraqi, Omani and Yemeni peasants who constitute the bulk of Kuwaiti manual labor.

## Palestine

Not all immigrants, however, are in this category: the majority of foreign workers emigrated for political reasons. The Arab-Israeli War of 1947 and the occupation of Palestine by Israeli forces resulted in 1,317,749 Arab refugees, distributed prior to the 1967 war as follows:

| | |
|---|---|
| Jordan | 706,568 |
| Gaza Strip | 307,245 |
| Lebanon | 163,904 |
| Syria | 140,032 |
| | 1,317,749 |

These figures do not include Palestinians who have lost their livelihood but not their homes, and who thus do not qualify for relief under the United Nations definition of 'refugees.' The self-supporting Palestinians number 54,000, distributed throughout the Arab world, Europe, and the USA.[8] *The New York Times* estimated the number of Palestinians outside Isreal to be 2.2 million, while 1.5 million Palestinians still live under Israeli occupation.[9]

During the early 1950s the number of Palestinians in Kuwait was 15,173; however, their number increased considerably during the following decade, as shown in Table 3.1.

**Table 3.1** *Palestinian and Jordanian population in Kuwait, census years 1957–75*

| | 1957 | 1961 | 1965 | 1970 | 1975 |
|---|---|---|---|---|---|
| Male | 11,616 | 25,741 | 49,744 | 79,934 | 107,770 |
| Female | 3,557 | 11,741 | 27,968 | 67,762 | 96,408 |
| Total | 15,173 | 37,482 | 77,712 | 147,696 | 204,178 |

Source: Ministry of Planning Board of Census, *Population Census 1957*; and *Annual Statistical Abstracts* 1964–75.

During the 1950s the number of Palestinians in Kuwait was relatively low, especially females. This is a reflection of the Arab world's limited interest in Kuwait before its independence in 1961. At any rate the Kuwaiti economy of that period would have been unable to absorb a high population of Palestinians. Kuwait was involved in building its capital and social infrastructure (roads, schools, hospitals) and there was a high demand for unskilled labor, which was provided by Iraqi and

Iranian laborers. Furthermore, the essential skilled manpower was provided by some Palestinians and Egyptians. After independence, the Kuwaiti economy expanded rapidly and the demand for qualified manpower increased considerably.

In the 1960s the number of Palestinians in Kuwait increased rapidly. The number of males doubled within a five-year period (1957–61); and the number of females tripled during that same time. Within two decades (1957–75), the number of males increased more than nine times; the number of females increased twenty-seven times. This tremendous increase in numbers stemmed from Palestinians who were homeless after 1948 and had settled in other Arab countries, moving to Kuwait because of both the employment possibilities and the freedom from political harassment and disputes with other governments–particularly Jordan, Syria, Lebanon, and Egypt. (It is also true that a consequence of the 1967 war was a greater political awareness among many young Palestinians.)

During the last twenty years, the number of Palestinians in Kuwait has increased many times, and they have become the largest community in Kuwait after the Kuwaiti nationals. (In 1975 they constituted 20.5 per cent of the total population.)

## Egypt

High unemployment and the implementation of socialism in Egypt are the major 'push' reasons for the Egyptian migration to Kuwait. Like other underdeveloped countries, Egypt experienced such problems as overpopulation, unemployment and under-employment.[10] These problems, combined with Egypt's socialist program in 1961, forced the many Egyptians who opposed socialism to seek employment in other, non-socialist oil-producing Arab states that offered higher wages. Table 3.2 indicates the size of the Egyptian labor force in Kuwait.

**Table 3.2**  *Egyptian population in Kuwait, census years 1957–75*

|          | 1957  | 1961            | 1965   | 1970   | 1975   |
|----------|-------|-----------------|--------|--------|--------|
| Male     | 858   | 11,857<br>(UAR) | 5,796  | 11,392 | 35,795 |
| Female   | 876   | 4,859           | 5,225  | 13,029 | 24,739 |
| Total    | 1,734 | 16,716          | 11,021 | 24,421 | 60,534 |

Source: Ministry of Planning Board of Census, *Population Census 1957*; and *Annual Statistical Abstracts* 1964, 1975.

*Foreign manpower*

The Egyptian population, unlike other Arab and non-Arab communities in Kuwait, has accounted for a large number of females ever since the beginning of emigration in the 1950s. This is explained by the great demand that existed for Egyptian females as teachers, nurses, doctors and social workers. The 1961 figures show a decline in the number of females but this census includes Syrians and Egyptians (the two countries were united from 1958 to 1961), and the exact number of Egyptians, male or female, during those years is extremely difficult to determine.

In the period from 1965 to 1975, the number of Egyptians emigrating to Kuwait increased more than five times, from 11,021 to 60,534. This high increase was due to the great demand for such high-level manpower as doctors, engineers and lawyers. The reasons for the relatively small increase in the number of Egyptian females was the intense competition from Palestinian and other Arab women who entered the labor force during the 1960s and 1970s.

## Iraq

Political instability and lack of economic development were the major 'push factors' for workers from Iraq and Iran. Although both countries are oil-producing and rich in agriculture, the number of workers from these two countries continues to increase, to the point where presently they constitute the fourth and fifth largest labor force in Kuwait.

Countries like Iraq, Iran, Oman and Saudi Arabia, which had manpower problems of their own, lost skilled and unskilled labor to other Gulf states, mainly Kuwait, and then attempted to import labor from other countries. Iraq, for example, initiated a program of resettlement for Egyptian peasants and their families in Iraq. The Egyptians coming to Iraq under this program were granted Iraqi nationality and worked at the Experimental Cooperative Farms. Iraq is expected to bring as many as 500,000 Egyptian peasants into the country.[11]

This migration to Kuwait was due to political instability in Iraq and the deterioration of the agricultural sector. Next to oil, agriculture is the most important sector of Iraq's economy; it represents approximately 20-5 per cent of the country's GNP. Furthermore, employment in the agricultural sector is the highest in the country with a total of 2,110,593 employees in 1971.[12] Currently, about 23 million dunums are utilized for agricultural purposes; however, a potential exists to cultivate 95 million dunums, which is equivalent to 238,000 square kilometers.[13]

During the monarchy of 1953–4, Iraq exported ID 14.4 million ($43.3 million) worth of foodstuffs; in 1959, under the Revolutionary Government, Iraq imported ID 93 million ($276 million). There are several reasons for the deterioration in agriculture, the major one being the political instability in Iraq since the 1958 revolution. The period 1958–65 witnessed three successful military takeovers and a number of unsuccessful ones. Moreover, during these seven years, there were sixteen cabinet changes.[14] This political instability had a profound effect on Iraq because its economic plans frequently changed with the regime. Since the 1958 revolution, the emphasis has shifted back and forth between agriculture and industry. During the period 1958–68, each ministry was to implement the Development Project. Between the years 1953–64, Iraq had eight Ministers of Industry and Transport and six Ministers of Agrarian Reform.[15] This political instability adversely affected employment in agriculture, and many peasants became either under-employed or unemployed; as one author expressed: 'Iraq is no different from other under-developed countries in the fact that this sector suffers from chronic underemployment and seasonal unemployment reaching as high as 75 to 80 percent.'[16] Because of the decline in agriculture and the high unemployment in this sector, many peasants migrated to the urban centers, particularly the capital, Baghdad, in central Iraq, Basra in the south, and Mosul to the north. When these migrants failed to find jobs in the cities, they left for the nearest country in which employment was available, which was Kuwait or one of the other oil-producing states in the Gulf.

Iraqi migrant labor in Kuwait forms the third largest group after the Palestinians and Egyptians. During the 1950s, they were one of the largest migrant groups in Kuwait. Their number declined for a while but then increased again.

Table 3.3. shows that the number of Iraqi workers declined from 27,148 in 1961 to 25,897 in 1965. This was primarily due to the

**Table 3.3**   *Iraqi population in Kuwait, census years 1957–75*

|        | 1957   | 1961   | 1965   | 1970   | 1975   |
|--------|--------|--------|--------|--------|--------|
| Male   | 18,728 | 16,702 | 15,762 | 23,583 | 26,499 |
| Female | 7,307  | 10,446 | 10,135 | 15,483 | 18,571 |
| Total  | 26,035 | 27,148 | 25,897 | 39,066 | 45,070 |

Source: Ministry of Planning, Board of Census, *Population Census 1957* and *Annual Statistical Abstracts* 1964–75

deterioration of relations between the two countries at the time. When Kuwait gained independence in 1961, Iraq claimed that Kuwait was not an independent state but part of Iraq. Kuwait took security measures by deporting some of the Iraqi workers. This hostile relationship between the two countries continued until 1963, when a new military takeover in Iraq overthrew the Qassem regime. The return to normal relations between the two countries and the introduction of socialism in Iraq increased Iraqi migration to Kuwait. The latest Iraqi migrants consist not only of unskilled workers but also of professional and skilled people who, for various reasons, cannot return to Iraq.

### Iran

Iran, like Iraq, suffers from political instability and lack of economic planning, especially in the agricultural sector. There was major political unrest in Iran in 1951 when the nationalist gvernment, led by Dr Muhammad Mossedegh, nationalized the Anglo-Iranian Oil Co.[17] This led to the ousting of the prime minister in 1953.[18] The continued absolute rule and control of the political system by the shah in Iran was one of the major obstacles to economic development. The shah's White Revolution in 1963 failed because of his intent to preserve rather than uproot the traditional patterns of patrimonialism that underlie Iranian socio-political relations.[19] Due to political instability and the lack of genuine economic development in Iran, many professional Iranians have emigrated to Europe and the USA. Moreoever, unskilled labor has emigrated to the Gulf states. By 1975 the Iranian population in Kuwait was the largest non-Arab community in the country.

The total Iranian population in Kuwait has increased yearly except in 1961 (table 3.4). Possible reasons for the decline in 1961 were the

**Table 3.4**   *Iranian population in Kuwait, census years 1957–75*

|          | 1957   | 1961   | 1965   | 1970   | 1975   |
|----------|--------|--------|--------|--------|--------|
| Male     | 18,378 | 16,681 | 29,025 | 35,498 | 33,359 |
| Female   | 1,541  | 1,567  | 1,765  | 3,631  | 7,483  |
| Total    | 19,919 | 18,248 | 30,790 | 39,129 | 40,842 |

Iranian fear that they were not welcome in Kuwait after independence, and the political instability in Kuwait subsequent to Iraq's claim to Kuwait. Table 3.4 also shows that the majority of Iranians are male and that the number of females is relatively small. The reason for this is that the majority of Iranians who come to Kuwait are peasants and traditionalists who believe that leaving the wife at home is safer and more economical, since a group of male workers can save money on rent by living together.

**Table 3.5**  *Population of Kuwait by sex and nationality, 1975*

| Nationality | Male | Female | Total | % |
|---|---|---|---|---|
| Kuwait | 236,600 | 235,488 | 472,088 | 47.5 |
| Jordan and | | | | |
| Palestine | 107,770 | 96,408 | 204,178 | 20.5 |
| Egypt | 35,795 | 24,739 | 60,534 | 6.1 |
| Iraq | 26,499 | 18,571 | 45,070 | 4.5 |
| Syria | 24,641 | 16,321 | 40,962 | 4.1 |
| Lebanon | 13,208 | 11,568 | 24,776 | 2.5 |
| Saudi Arabia | 6,620 | 5,907 | 12,527 | 1.3 |
| South Yemen | 10,311 | 2,021 | 12,332 | 1.2 |
| North Yemen | 3,755 | 1,076 | 4,831 | 0.5 |
| Oman | 5,117 | 2,196 | 7,313 | 0.7 |
| Other Arabs | 3,709 | 2,955 | 6,664 | 0.7 |
| Total Arab | 474,025 | 417,250 | 891,275 | 89.6 |
| Iran | 33,359 | 7,483 | 40,842 | 4.1 |
| India | 16,779 | 15,326 | 32,105 | 3.2 |
| Pakistan | 14,996 | 8,020 | 23,016 | 2.3 |
| England | 1,293 | 1,130 | 2,423 | 0.2 |
| USA | 351 | 343 | 694 | 0.1 |
| Other nationalities | 2,713 | 1,451 | 4,164 | 0.5 |
| Total non-Arab | 69,743 | 33,819 | 103,562 | 10.4 |
| Grand Total | 543,768 | 451,069 | 994,834 | 100.0 |

Source: Ministry of Planning, *Annual Statistical Abstract 1976*, table 17.

## Profile of the foreign labor force in Kuwait

Foreign labor migration has been a crucial concern of several European organizations and agencies, and various studies have been conducted concerning the social, economic, and political impact on the 'host' and source countries. The general laws and regulations concerning the foreign labor force in Kuwait will be examined, and the occupations they perform will be explained.

The total number of foreigners in Kuwait according to the 1980 census was 793,762 persons; of these, 497,609 were male, and 296,153 were female. Non-Kuwaitis accounted for 58.5 per cent of the population.

*Foreign manpower*

The majority of the migrant population has come from Arab and Muslim countries, which is important because those migrant laborers adjust more easily in a traditional society such as Kuwait. Those who come from a socially similar background, such as Saudi Arabia and the Gulf states, adjust more easily.

Table 3.6 shows the median stay of the foreign labor force in Kuwait. The people most likely to reside longer are those able to adjust socially

**Table 3.6** *Foreign labor force and median stay in Kuwait, by nationality*

| Rank | Nationality | Median stay (years) |
|------|-------------|---------------------|
| 1 | Gulf emirates | 7.9 |
| 2 | Saudi Arabia | 7.4 |
| 3 | Lebanon | 6.9 |
| 4 | Iraq | 6.6 |
| 5 | Pakistan | 6.5 |
| 6 | Oman | 6.3 |
| 7 | Yemen Arab Republic | 5.7 |
| 8 | Jordan and Palestine | 5.7 |
| 9 | India | 5.4 |
| 10 | UK | 5.2 |
| 11 | Syria | 5.0 |
| 12 | Iran | 4.8 |
| 13 | South Yemen | 4.7 |
| 14 | Egypt | 3.6 |
| 15 | Western European Countries | 2.6 |
| | Total Arab countries | 5.8 |
| | Total non-Arab countries | 5.3 |
| | Grand Total | 5.7 |

Source: M.S. Al Akhrass, *The Study of Labor Force Residency*, Arab Planning Institute, Kuwait, 1976.

to Kuwait. An important aspect of the table is that the Lebanese rank third; it is a nation of migrants and a large percentage of Lebanese (78 per cent) either have their own business or work for a private company.[20]

The highest turnover or shortest stay in Kuwait is among the Western Europeans and Egyptians. The reason for this is that people from these countries come on a contract basis and leave as soon as their contract expires. Qualified workers are unlikely to stay for an extended period, because of the wage differential between the Kuwaiti and the non-Kuwaiti population.

The movement of migrants into Kuwait differs from that in Europe, where labor moves from economically backward countries such as Spain, Turkey and Italy to more advanced countries such as Germany, France and Switzerland. In Kuwait, labor comes from countries such as Saudi Arabia, United Arab Emirates, Iraq and Iran; most of these countries are wealthier than Kuwait.

Unlike Europe, where foreign workers take only the socially undesirable jobs,[21] in Kuwait foreigners are distributed throughout diverse occupations (see chapter 2). Moreover, Kuwait can be distinguished from Europe where 'employment of foreigners spreads progressively from primitive pockets of poverty to other jobs.'[22]

In Kuwait, employment and demand for foreign workers initially came from the top. The need for high-level manpower has progressed evenly with that for manual labor. During the early 1950s, manpower was in such demand in Kuwait that the government offered qualified foreigners the incentives of high wages, furnished housing and a car.[23] These incentives did not work, however; a resentment developed amongst the Kuwaiti population, particularly amongst the few qualified and educated Kuwaitis, who felt that they were not being given the same benefits as their foreign equals.

Among the foreign labor force in Kuwait, a division of labor exists; the majority of the Iranian and Iraqi labor force, for example, is employed as sales, service and production workers, while many of the Egyptians and Palestinians work as professionals and government employees (see table 3.7). Furthermore, many are employed as production and machinery workers. Pakistanis and Indians tend to work as skilled workers in technical jobs. Table 3.7 shows that the Palestinians and Jordanians outnumber other groups in every occupation except service, agriculture and production. The highest concentration of Palestinians after production is professional and governmental executive employees, 37.5 per cent and 31 per cent respectively. In the production and machinery field, the figure is 19.9 per cent. Thus, there are more Palestinians in high-level occupations than in low-level occupations; this fact, together with their large number, make the Palestinians the most influential single community in Kuwait, and Kuwait is one of the strongest supporters of the Palestine Liberation Organization (for example, Kuwait stopped payments to Jordan in September 1970 when they crushed the Palestinian commandos there).[24]

Most of the PLO leadership worked in Kuwait until the formation of Fatah in 1965. The Palestinians residing in Kuwait pay a 5 per cent monthly tax to the PLO. The collection of this tax and other

**Table 3.7** Non-Kuwaiti labor force, by nationality and major occupational group, 1975 (over 15 years old)

| Major occupational groups | Iraq | Jordan and Palestine | Egypt | Syria | Lebanon | Iran | India | Pakistan | USA and Western Europe | Others | Grand total |
|---|---|---|---|---|---|---|---|---|---|---|---|
| Professional, technical and related workers | 1,007 | 12,052 | 11,061 | 1,376 | 1,055 | 246 | 2,602 | 730 | 974 | 1,021 | 32,097 |
| Administrative and managerial workers | 100 | 562 | 241 | 102 | 169 | 23 | 177 | 68 | 315 | 52 | 1,809 |
| Government executive clerical and related workers | 1,404 | 8,327 | 2,309 | 744 | 757 | 384 | 2,672 | 762 | 204 | 1,100 | 20,166 |
| Sales workers | 912 | 3,795 | 740 | 2,637 | 1,053 | 3,394 | 1,729 | 380 | 71 | 4,797 | 17,908 |
| Service workers | 4,919 | 4,086 | 8,338 | 2,496 | 816 | 4,308 | 10,546 | 1,781 | 62 | 8,048 | 45,400 |
| Agricultural workers, animal breeders, fishermen | 1,246 | 893 | 436 | 309 | 12 | 464 | 9 | 61 | 6 | 369 | 3,805 |
| Production, machinery and related workers | 8,411 | 17,938 | 14,383 | 8,884 | 3,373 | 20,114 | 2,740 | 7,256 | 107 | 7,054 | 90,260 |
| Total | 17,999 | 47,653 | 37,558 | 16,548 | 7,232 | 28,933 | 21,475 | 11,038 | 1,846 | 22,483 | 211,444 |

Source: *Population Census 1975*, Govt. Printing, 1975, vol. II, table 95; see also *Annual Statistical Abstract 1976*.

contributions is executed with assistance from the Kuwaiti government. The Palestinians in Kuwait are a significant group. Directly and indirectly they influence the government's internal and external policies. For example, in the summer of 1976 the Kuwaiti government supported the Syrian move into Lebanon to counter Iraq, with whom Kuwait had a border dispute. However, the government, through its support of the Syrian move into Lebanon, found itself in a dilemma since the press – one of the major supporters of the PLO – was strongly against the Syrian and right-wing Lebanese co-operation in Lebanon. Most of the editors in the Kuwaiti press are Palestinians.[25]

The second most important group after the Palestinians is the Egyptians. Their importance derives from their large number of qualified workers, especially in the field of education. In 1976-7, for example, there were 3,583 Egyptian male teachers and 3,874 female teachers, a total of 7,457. This is significant when we consider that the total number of teachers at that time was 18,227, putting the proportion of Egyptian teachers at 40.9 per cent.[26] At Kuwait University, 178 of a total of 341 academic staff are Egyptian, some 52.2 per cent.[27] Because of the large number of Egyptians in the Ministry of Education the education system in Kuwait is patterned after that of Egypt. Through its unique relationship with Egypt, Kuwait assured itself that Egyptian teachers would continue to work in Kuwait.[28] In point of fact, Kuwait's neutral stand in the Arab cold war has helped it maintain the flow of manpower necessary to its development.

The third largest Arab community in Kuwait is the Iraqi community. Most intermarriages between Kuwaiti and non-Kuwaiti are between Kuwaitis and Iraqis.[29] They are very similar and can often trace their origins from the same tribe.

The largest non-Arab group in Kuwait is the Iranian labor force. However, although one of the largest, its impact on Kuwaiti society remains marginal because the jobs available are among the lowest on the occupational ladder. Many of these Iranian/Persian workers have entered the country illegally and are therefore subject to exploitation. Most accept low-paying jobs and may be deported at any time.

## Legal and economic conditions of the foreign labor force

To improve work and productivity, priority must be given to the social, economic and legal conditions of migrant manpower, which represents 75 per cent of the labor force in Kuwait. When the demand for qualified manpower was very high, during the early period of Kuwait's development in the late 1940s and early 1950s, the government provided incentives to work in Kuwait. These incentives included relatively high wages, rent-free homes with utilities and water paid by the government, and, in some instances, a car and chauffeur. However, in the early 1960s, the supply of workers began to exceed the demand.

Such incentives were provided for high-level manpower only and the unskilled foreign labor force was paid comparatively very low salaries. The International Bank missions in Kuwait reported that the daily rate for workers was KD 0.75 ($2.55).[30]

Despite favorable treatment during the 1950s, the non-Kuwaitis were never treated on equal footing with their Kuwaiti counterparts. For example, Kuwaiti employees were provided with social security and retirement benefits; non-Kuwaitis were denied this right. This policy continues despite recommendations from the World Bank and Stanford Research Institute.[31] The present system of social security, created on September 2, 1976, applies exclusively to Kuwaiti nationals.[32]

Kuwaiti citizens have priority over their non-Kuwaiti counterparts in the field of employment, and clear distinctions exist in relation to other public facilities. Lack of equal opportunity for the advancement of foreign workers is widespread. Although the non-Kuwaiti labor force is distributed among the various occupational groups, they are still paid less than their Kuwaiti counterparts, even though they are frequently better qualified. A Kuwaiti school guard, for example, will often have a monthly salary three times that of an Arab high-school teacher who teaches 48 hours per week.[33] Furthermore, the Kuwaiti guards are usually illiterate, while foreign teachers must have a BA or BSc degree to teach in Kuwait.

This discrimination against the non-Kuwaiti is evident in the government's average salary distribution (see table 3.8). Moreover, the salary structure in the public sector is not designed to encourage effective utilization of scarce skills.

It should be said, however, that not all foreigners receive lower salaries than the Kuwaitis; many have highly-paid, responsible positions in the government and private sectors. For example, at Kuwait University the foreign professors receive higher salaries than the Kuwaiti professors; furthermore, they are provided with such benefits as free housing and free air tickets.

Foreigners in Kuwait cannot own real property or open businesses without a Kuwaiti partner or 'Kafeel' guardian who will register the establishment in his name. The Kuwaiti 'Kafeel' usually collects an

**Table 3.8** *Average government salary*

| Total monthly salary (KD) | Kuwaiti (%) 1972 | 1976 | non-Kuwaiti (%) 1972 | 1976 |
|---|---|---|---|---|
| Less than 70 | 0.15 | 1.1 | 2.71 | 35.1 |
| 70 | 0.02 | 0.6 | 0.87 | 5.6 |
| 80 | 0.11 | 5.4 | 3.16 | 9.8 |
| 100 | 0.77 | 4.2 | 6.08 | 8.9 |
| 120 | 10.04 | 13.1 | 16.53 | 13.2 |
| 150 | 46.60 | 27.7 | 40.28 | 8.9 |
| 200 | 28.32 | 26.1 | 18.09 | 10.1 |
| 250 | 8.07 | 13.4 | 7.38 | 4.3 |
| 300 | 2.78 | 4.3 | 2.35 | 2.0 |
| 350 | 0.97 | 2.2 | 0.84 | 0.9 |
| 400 | 0.64 | 0.8 | 0.51 | 0.5 |
| 450 | 0.16 | 0.3 | 0.30 | 0.2 |
| 500 | 0.71 | 0.4 | 0.59 | 0.3 |
| 600 | 0.58 | 0.4 | 0.31 | 0.2 |
| Total | 100 | 100 | 100 | 100 |

Source: Planning Board, Bureau of Census, *Census of Government Employees 1972* (Arabic), p. 38; *Annual Statistical Abstract 1979*, p. 144, table 135.

agreed-upon annual payment or part of the profit, depending on the particular contract. This 'Alkafala' system was undoubtedly created to prevent competition of foreign entrepreneurs with the Kuwaiti merchant class. The main beneficiary is the Kuwaiti merchant or employer.

The Kafeel system is frequently abused by the merchant or employer. For example, if a Kuwaiti national is interested in an Indian or Pakistani cook or driver, he initially contacts the Indian/Pakistani community and correspondence is then established to find such a person. After agreement upon a salary, the Kuwaiti employer agrees to pay for the travel allowance. When the prospective employee arrives in Kuwait, he or she is *obliged* to remain in the service of that person up to the time agreed upon in his or her contract, which is normally two years. In certain ways, this system is similar to 'indentured servitude,' since the employed person is forced by law to remain with the employer, regardless of the particular working conditions. In other words, the employee is prevented legally from seeking other employment.

A new regulation recently issued by the Ministry of the Interior states the following in Article 3, concerning the private servant: 'If the servant leaves his employer before the expiration of the contract, the residency permit will not be given to him unless his employer agrees to it. . . .'[34] If foreigners do not have a residency permit or a job, they are subject to immediate deportation.

Another area where discrimination exists is trade unions. Article 72 of the Labor Law in the private sector prohibits non-Kuwaiti workers from forming a trade union;[35] however, the law allows them to join a Kuwaiti trade union after serving five years on one job. Foreigners are not allowed, however, to vote or run for office in a union.

The widespread discrimination against the non-Kuwaiti labor force is one of the major disputes between the government and the Kuwaiti Trade Union. If non-Kuwaitis were allowed to organize a trade union, working conditions would improve considerably for both non-Kuwaiti and Kuwaiti workers alike. A non-Kuwaiti trade union would result in minimum or standard wages for all, Kuwaiti and non-Kuwaiti. Moreover, the Kuwaiti worker could negotiate wage increases without the threat that he might be replaced by a non-Kuwaiti who would work for lower wages.

The government decision to prevent non-Kuwaiti workers from organizing themselves was both politically and economically motivated. The government believed that if the non-Kuwaitis organized themselves then the labor movement in Kuwait could become a strong political force — an intolerable situation. Furthermore, if the non-Kuwaitis organized themselves they would demand better salaries and living conditions. To date, neither the government nor the merchant society has been willing to grant these rights. The primary reason that the foreign workers in Kuwait have not demanded to form a union for themselves (in addition to the fact that the government has not allowed them to do so) is that they represent more than twenty nations, each with a different type of society and cultural background. Most of these people are from various Arab countries in which trade unionism continues to be either unimportant or an instrument of the state.[36]

Although foreigners in Kuwait are not organized in unions, they periodically lead spontaneous strikes. In 1974, for example, Kuwait witnessed several labor strikes; two were led by non-union foreign workers who in September demanded that Kinko, a Kuwait oil-supply company, reduce the number of working hours from eight to six during the holy month of Ramadan. (During the month of Ramadan working hours in all government ministries are shortened to four hours instead of six.) Essentially, these workers, were requesting the same basic right as other workers, such as the Kuwaiti muslims. Another strike took place in September 1974 by soft-drink workers (Canada Dry Company), demanding better working conditions and an increase in salary to meet the high cost of living.[37]

Even in housing a clear distinction exists between Kuwaitis and non-Kuwaitis.[38] The newly built suburb of Kuwait is exclusively for Kuwaiti nationals; the non-Kuwaitis live in the old city of Kuwait and in some of the older suburbs such as Hawalli and Salmyia. Since foreigners in Kuwait do not have the right to own property, they rent apartments and houses in the 'left-over' areas, such as Kuwait City. Furthermore, the exclusively Kuwaiti district usually offers more services, such as a co-operative food society, which is reserved for Kuwaitis only, better telephone and electricity services, and newly constructed schools and polytechnics.

Because the shortage of housing is so severe in Kuwait, directly and indirectly affecting the foreign labor force, it is essential to discuss the problem in a more detailed fashion. With the discovery of oil and the arrival of a large immigrant population Kuwait City became over-crowded. As a solution the government decided upon an urbanization program. In 1952, the land-purchase program was initiated, by which the government purchased land inside Kuwait City from the merchants and other people. The government bought the land at inflated prices in order to spread the income from oil among the population. The land was used both for the building of roads and other public facilities, and for reselling to the private sector at extremely low prices.[39] In fact the major beneficiaries of this program were the land-owning classes, since they owned most of the land inside Kuwait City.

The World Bank Mission of 1961–3 criticized the program and recommended that expenditure be substantially reduced.[40]

This type of shortsighted policy has hindered the development of productive investment. Furthermore, this particular action inflated the price of land considerably:[41]

> When the government first began buying land for development in
> Shuwaikh, now an industrial area west of Kuwait City, it was paying
> under half a rupee per square foot, but by the mid 1950's the price
> had risen to R500, and by the early 1960's in the present centre of
> the city it reached K.D. 55, which means that the space required to
> park a car costs $19,600.

Since 1973 high oil prices and economic uncertainty in Europe, especially in England, have forced Kuwaiti merchants to bring money *back* to Kuwait to be invested in land speculation and in the Kuwaiti stock market. Consequently, the value of land has increased to the extent that 750 square meters of land in the desert outside Kuwait City and the suburbs cost anywhere between $150,000 and $200,000. This substantial increase in the price of land in turn has led to increases in rent, which landlords claim are necessary to attain appropriate value from their investment. The average rent for a modest apartment is now in excess of KD200 or $678 per month;[42] and the rent for a centrally air-conditioned apartment ranges anywhere between KD400 and DK800 per month ($1,400 and $2,800). The workers who have most recently arrived in Kuwait are most affected by these increases; rent typically constitutes about 60 per cent of their salary.

Many landlords have recently terminated leases or attempted to evacuate their non-Kuwaiti tenants under the pretext of reconstruction; instead, they prepare the apartment for new tenants who are willing to pay two or three times as much rent for the same apartment. However, the government quickly passed regulations which — under any conditions — prohibited further increases in rent and the eviction of tenants. Whilst these government regulations protect those workers who are already living in Kuwait, it is difficult to predict to what extent they will assist those new workers that the government is attempting to attract.

The Ministry of Education requires a minimum number of teachers and administrators for the academic year. For 1977–8, 4,000 new teachers and administrators were required.[43] Because these teachers will not leave their home countries unless housing is ensured at a reasonable cost, the government is attempting to alleviate the problem by subsidizing housing for newly arriving professional workers. In 1976 the government allocated $3,390 million for 51,000 new homes of every description to be built over a five-year period.[44]

A primary reason for the housing shortage in Kuwait is the government's entry into the market. The government rents buildings and houses for its various ministries and its foreign employees, and many landlords prefer to rent their apartments to the government rather than to individuals. This housing shortage could have been reduced substantially if the government had built its own houses for its employees instead of renting them from the landlords, who in turn increased the rent. It is worth pointing out that in spite of the close link between the speculators, real estate and the stock market on the one hand, and the power structure on the other, the government's decision to build houses for its employees was strongly opposed by the merchants, who claimed that excessive government intervention in the market was one cause of the shortage.[45] Eventually, the government succumbed to this pressure and gradually diminished its program of building houses for its employees. Again, the victims of this housing shortage was the middle-class

Kuwaitis and such skilled non-Kuwaiti workers as technicians, electricians and machinists; the government provided only for the low-income Kuwaitis (monthly income of less than KD 150 or $510), with low-income houses. In 1952, fourteen low-income houses were built; in 1964, the total reached 4,662; and in 1975, the total number was 14,961. The total number of applications under consideration in 1976 was 20,049.[46]

The phrase 'welfare state' is frequently used in relation to Kuwait. This phrase is extremely misleading. The reality is that in one of the richest oil-producing countries there are 12,425 shacks and provisional dwellings inhabited by Kuwaiti nationals and 6,181 shacks inhabited by non-Kuwaitis.

The government provides the Kuwaiti middle class with land and interest-free loans amounting to KD 25,000 ($85,000). The cost of building a simple house in Kuwait ranges anywhere between KD 30,000 and 60,000 ($102,000 and $204,000). Therefore, a newly graduated Kuwaiti can rarely build a house without a government loan and/or assistance from his family.

As a rule, a high-level, non-Kuwaiti worker is provided with housing by his employer, while his unskilled counterpart lives in an old house in groups or in shacks or tents at the construction site.

The housing shortage and high inflation has affected the immigrant workers more severely than the indigenous population: 'Inflation, disguised in the official figures by subsidies which often only apply to Kuwaitis, had made life increasingly hard for immigrant workers. This was particularly so in the field of housing where rising building costs produced acute shortages and astronomic prices.'[47]

Further discrimination is evident between Kuwaitis and non-Kuwaitis in education. Historically, education in Kuwait has been free for every child; however, during the last decade it has become impossible to continue this policy because of the tremendous increase in foreigners. Due to an apparent lack of facilities, the government gave priority to the children of Kuwaiti citizens, followed by the children of Arabs employed by the government. The government's argument is that not enough space exists to accommodate all newcomers in the existing government schools. (Further details are given in chapter 4.)

Certain jobs in Kuwait can only be filled by Kuwaiti citizens. For example, in 1964 a law was passed which stipulated that only Kuwaiti lawyers could register in the Kuwait Lawyer's Association. The non-Kuwaiti lawyer cannot defend a client in court without special permission from the Minister of Justice; moreover, he needs to be accompanied by a registered Kuwaiti lawyer during the defense of his particular case in court.[48]

Discrimination against the foreign population in Kuwait is evident in numerous other ways. As discussed, non-Kuwaitis are denied equal rights and opportunities in the fields of employment, business and the ownership of property. However, the situation extends even to food co-operatives and sport. Although the non-Kuwaiti population is allowed to shop and spend its money in these co-operatives, it cannot achieve membership. The profit, therefore, is divided among the Kuwaiti members only, despite the fact that most customers are non-Kuwaiti. It is interesting to note that, as in other sectors of the economy, most employees in the co-operatives are foreign. Furthermore, those Kuwaitis employed in the co-operatives are mainly employed in the management sections.[49]

Although non-Kuwaitis are allowed to join the various sports clubs, they are prevented from participating in the various national sports. The official Kuwaiti justification for this exclusion is that they need to develop the potential Kuwaiti players; if non-Kuwaitis were allowed to join the national leagues, the potential of the Kuwaitis would suffer in the process.[50]

## Uncertainty in Kuwait

There is growing uncertainty in Kuwait over the implications of the overdependence on foreign labor and on how 'the non-Kuwaitis who were brought into the country to supplement the labor force ended up dominating it.'[51] To evaluate change in Kuwait is difficult; and to assess the foreign contribution to such change is even more complex. Because the immigrant communities in Kuwait came from widely divergent cultural backgrounds, they were bound to influence the host country's population, and especially when they constituted the majority of the population.

The foreign presence has affected Kuwait's economic, social and political system. From an economic standpoint, Kuwait could not have reached its current stage of development without the assistance of its foreign labor force (see chapter 2). The foreign labor force is the backbone of the Kuwaiti economy and it constitutes 75 per cent of the total labor force. Its economic importance cannot be under-estimated. The Palestinians and Egyptians have dominated the fields of medicine and education,[52] and in fact if the Egyptians decided to withdraw from Kuwait, the educational system would be likely to come to a standstill.

Socially, the presence of foreigners has altered many of the traditional habits and customs. Before the discovery of oil, women in Kuwait were not allowed to socialize with men — basically, they were restricted to the home. However, the influx of foreign women into the labor force strongly contributed to the process of liberating the Kuwaiti female population. Furthermore, socialization, in schools, where most of the teachers are Arabs (from Egypt, Palestine, Jordan, Syria and Iraq), has had an impact on the youth of Kuwait. Kuwaiti society has borrowed and incorporated much from Indian customs and habits as well. This influence has been strongest in the Kuwaiti adaptation of Indian dishes and spices; Kuwaiti music is also much influenced by African and Indian music.[53]

The foreign influence has also extended to the judicial system: 'The judicial system, while theoretically based on Shari Law, is in practice based on a legal code adopted from the Egyptian Code, which itself was largely based on European Law.'[54]

In terms of education, foreign influence has been extensive. Due to the considerable talent and assistance of Arab teachers, the Kuwaiti educational system has been transformed from a relatively simple one, based on religion, to a comprehensive and modern system (see chapter 4).

Foreign influence has also been significant in the field of administration. Prior to the discovery of oil, the affairs of state were handled by the ruler (Amir), who was assisted by tribal leaders who solved community disputes on a personal basis.

As indicated earlier, one of the most significant changes has been the tremendous increase of population in Kuwait.[55] The Kuwaiti population at the beginning of this century was estimated by the World Bank to be between 10,000 and 12,000 people. In 1937 the population reached 75,000.[56] With the discovery of oil and the influx of a foreign labor force, the population of Kuwait jumped to a record figure. In 1957 the population reached 206,473; in 1961 it was 321,621; by 1965, 467,339; by 1970, 738,662; and finally, in 1975, the population reached 994,837. The growth rate in Kuwait has been the highest in the world, with an average annual increase of 9.8 per cent (see chapter 2, table 2.2).

This demographic trend brought resentment toward non-Kuwaitis, who were viewed by many Kuwaitis as 'coming to take our money and leave.' However, some Kuwaitis argued that the presence of a large number of non-Kuwaitis was a positive influence: 'The fact remains that the entry of the non-Kuwaitis has had a profound effect on the

Kuwaiti way of life, and one of its positive aspects is its contribution to fostering a type of solidarity among the Kuwaitis themselves — solidarity which characterizes every minority in the world.'[57]

Historically, urbanization in the west has been directly related to modernization. As stated by Inkeles and Smith: 'The defining features of a modern nation are then taken to include mass education, urbanization, industrialization, bureaucratization, and rapid communication.'[58] Daniel Lerner argued that with urbanization the modernizing process begins: 'The secular education of a participant society appears to involve a regular sequence of three phases. Urbanization comes first, for cities alone have developed the complex of skills and resources which characterize the modern industrial economy.'[59]

In many less developed countries, including Kuwait, Lerner's statement can be challenged since, like other Middle East countries, Kuwait achieved urbanization without development. Urbanization in Kuwait is developing rapidly, and one author considers the rate of urbanization in Kuwait to be one of the fastest not only in the Middle East but in the entire world.[60] This rapid process of urbanization in Kuwait is due primarily to the discovery of oil and the influx of immigrants. Most migrants reside in such urban centers as Kuwait City, Ahmadi City, Hawalli, and Salmiya. Thus in Kuwait, as in other Middle East countries, urbanization has not been followed by urbanism. As stated by Ibrahim: 'Most of the Arab countries have an over-population residing in their major cities. But the life styles of most are still rural and traditional. The segment which truly may be described as having an urbanistic modern life style does not exceed 30–40 percent of the urban population.'[61]

Another significant change in Kuwaiti society has been in terms of social composition. Before the discovery of oil, Kuwaiti society was a simple and traditional one, in which the tribal and clan relationship was very strong. It was divided into two major classes: (1) the upper class, consisting of the ruling families and the merchant society, and (2) the working class, which, before the discovery of oil, consisted of pearl-divers, carpenters, boat-builders, fishermen and farmers. Most of the working class were poor, illiterate and extremely dependent on the merchants for work. Generally, they were overworked and underpaid (see chapter 1 for further details). Before the discovery of oil, the working class in Kuwait was in the majority; however, with the discovery of oil Kuwaiti society witnessed the rise of the middle classes.

In western Europe and in the USA, the rise of the middle classes has been related to the process of industrialization. Similarly, the rise of the middle classes in Kuwait was primarily due to the discovery of oil and to the expansion of Kuwait's economy. The current middle class in Kuwait consists of teachers, engineers, doctors, small shopowners and civil employees.

The distinction between the Middle East middle class and that of other societies has been described by Halpern as follows:[62]

> The Middle East moved into the modern administrative age before it reached the machine age. Its salaried middle class attained power before it attained assurance of status, order, security or prosperity. In the Middle East, the salaried new middle class therefore uses its power not to defend order and property but to create them, a revolutionary task that is undertaken so far without any final commitment to any particular system or institutions.

The middle class in Kuwait attained its position not only through family ties and tribal affiliations but through the acquisition of education and technical skills. The middle class is very conscientious; it allies itself with the working class and supports many social, political and economic changes related to the working class. Furthermore, the middle class in Kuwait supports and participates in various Arab nationalist parties, such as the Arab Ba'ath Socialist Party or the Arab Nationalist movement.

The middle class in Kuwait tends to be progressive. One reason for this is that many of them feel that they are better qualified than the administrators or managers, who are not usually chosen from the middle or working classes. The new middle class is growing in importance due primarily to its high educational background. In the Kuwaiti Cabinet there are now at least five ministers who belong to the middle classes. They have acquired their position through education and through climbing the bureaucratic ladder.

The presence of a large population of non-Kuwaiti Arabs — mainly the Palestinian Arabs — has changed the Kuwaiti political outlook from a regionalist-orientated perspective to a Pan-Arab Nationalist viewpoint. The Arab Nationalist movement was founded during the early 1950s by a group of students at the American University of Beirut. Initially, the movement's objective was to achieve Arab unity in order to recover Palestine. In its early stages, the movement supported President Nasser of Egypt; however, after the 1967 defeat, it drifted to the left of the political spectrum. By late 1967, the Arab Nationalist movement organized the Popular Front for the Liberation of Palestine and adopted marxism as its doctrine.[63] The PFLP is dedicated to the destruction of Zionism and to the removal of Arab reactionary governments.

The Arab Nationalist movement is extremely active in Kuwait. Prior to independence when the British, French and Israelis attacked Egypt in 1956, the Kuwaiti Arab Nationalists sabotaged the oil facilities and demonstrated in support of Nasser and Arab Nationalism.[64] Members of the Arab Nationalist movement in Kuwait include six deputies in Kuwait's National Assembly led by Dr Ahmad Al Khatib, who formed the backbone of Kuwaiti opposition and was one of the original founders. They are very popular, especially among student organizations and the Kuwaiti labor unions.

One of the reasons for Kuwait's neutral policy in the Arab cold war (revolutionary versus reactionary) relates to the large non-Kuwaiti Arab population. Historically, Kuwait has often blamed its internal problems on the 'outside element' (i.e., foreigners) in Kuwait. Shaikh Mubarak Al Sabah (1896-1915) blamed two Egyptian scholars for stirring the population against the British in 1914.[65]

## Summary

The government's policy of making a distinction between the Kuwaiti and non-Kuwaiti population is undoubtedly taken as a defensive measure; more privileges are given to its own citizens who have become a minority within their own country.[66] This policy has had adverse effects. The Kuwaiti population has begun to perceive itself as a special people who do not need to work:[67]

> It could lead young Kuwaitis to grow up expecting that the higher standard of living than that of their non-Kuwaiti neighbours is *theirs* as a right, whether or not they contribute a personal effort to the wealth and well-being of Kuwaiti society as a whole. For a society which needs to build up now the manpower and technical resources that will operate the economy in an era when oil funds flow less freely, the widespread conviction that income is obtainable without commensurate effort is psychologically dangerous.

The danger of overdependence on others has been stressed: 'The dangers of an affluent minority reluctant to take on work of a non-white-collar nature and catered for by an underprivileged majority of foreigners needs hardly be emphasized.'[68] The policy of making a distinction between Kuwaiti and non-Kuwaiti has a negative impact on both the economy and the general political stability of the country.

The Kuwaiti government, in response to complaints from the foreign population, simply suggests they can move elsewhere. Such an argument may have been inconsequential during the initial stages of development when the majority of the foreign labor force was employed in the construction and service areas only. However, Kuwait's current dependence on the foreign labor force cannot be overstated.

Unequal access to social services for the foreign population has been more easily tolerated than the inequality of pay for equal work, which occurs in both the public and private sectors.[69] This inequality between the two populations has led many professionals such as doctors, engineers, and skilled workers, to leave Kuwait in favor of other countries that offer more equality.

Since 1973 the Kuwaiti press has been reporting on the shortage of manpower and on the emigration of non-Kuwaitis (mostly professionals) who are leaving in favor of other Arab oil-producing states, such as Libya, in which the expatriate labor force receives higher salaries than the native Libyans. The departure of professionals and skilled workers is becoming a serious problem in Kuwait, as stated in a Stanford Research Institute report: 'this study has determined that there is a constant flow of workers and technically trained personnel out of Kuwait. . . reaching some three thousand a year at least in the last category.'[70]

The treatment of the non-Kuwaitis is unlikely to improve considerably over the next decade. There will be a tendency for them to become less efficient and careless about work or to seek alternative opportunities in other countries of the region. In both cases Kuwait will be the loser. In 1977, inefficiency in government bureaucracy reached a crisis stage, which prompted the government to form a committee to study the reform of the bureaucracy. This committee comprised ministers of state and various officials in the government; it also included American management experts.[71] True reform and more efficiency in the bureaucracy cannot occur unless there is equality of treatment and pay for all workers, regardless of country of origin.

# Chapter 4

# Education and manpower

Highly qualified manpower is considered one of the most important groups, and many developed and underdeveloped countries constantly attempt to increase their share of high-level manpower. Economists were the first to regard 'human resources' as capital. Schultz considers education as an investment in man and he treats it as a form of capital.[1] Becker believes a positive relationship exists between a high level of education and positive incremental rates of return.[2] Harbison uses the term 'human capital formation' in relation to the 'process of acquiring and increasing the number of persons who have the skills, education, and experience which are critical for the economic and political development of the country.'[3] The importance of education for economic development has been expressed in the following words:[4]

> The underdeveloped countries are underdeveloped because most of their people are underdeveloped, having had no opportunity for expanding their potential capacities in the service of society . . . underdeveloped societies are underdeveloped because they are not geared to the types of activity which development entails and one of these is education in a general sense of the word.

Throughout countries of the Third World, including Kuwait, special emphasis is devoted to education. Many in these countries believe education will solve the manpower problem. The needs of the less developed countries for skilled and professional people require a substantial change in the quality and efficiency of educational and training programs so that they can be sure that the right kinds of people are prepared for the skills and professions that fit the labor market and social requirement.[5]

This chapter reviews the educational system of Kuwait, where the policy-makers emphasize the role of education; or, as stated by the Planning Board:[6]

> The plan aims at developing human resources by building up technical skills and scientific knowledge, by spread of education, by developing the potential abilities of the population and raising their productive efficiency through planned education and training and by raising the standards of health and culture of all.

This intense emphasis on education is an attempt to overcome the shortage of skills and professional manpower.

Kuwait, unlike many countries in the Gulf, introduced education prior to the discovery of oil; in fact, the first school in Kuwait opened in 1912, through the generous contributions of the merchant society. This first school was a private school limited to males only. The school was named Al-Mubarakia after the ruler of Kuwait — Mubarak Al-Sabah. Before the opening of this school, education was confined to the religious schools spread throughout the country. From the beginning in 1912 Arab scholars from Egypt and Tunisia supported the school, and introduced other subjects besides religion, such as Arabic history and mathematics.[7]

The second school opened in 1921. Since it was private, however, the number of pupils was limited. In 1936, the first Board of Education was elected, by prominent Kuwaitis. The board's initial responsibility was to send a letter to a judge in Palestine requesting him to send four teachers to Kuwait. In 1937, the Palestinian teachers arrived and public schools opened for the first time in Kuwait — both males and females.[8]

Quantitatively, education has made substantial advances. In the past twenty-five years enrollment in public schools has risen from 6,292 to 138,747 students, an increase of 2,205 per cent. Enrollment of male students over the period 1956–76 increased dramatically — from 15,946 to 127,380, an increase of 798.8 per cent. The number of female students during this same period rose by 1,256.9 per cent. Thus although the number of male students increased eight times, the number of female students increased more than twelve times during the same period. Table 4.1 shows that female enrollment began more slowly than male enrollment, but that it has accelerated to such a degree during recent years that the original disparity no longer exists. Furthermore, since 1972 the number of female teachers has been greater than the number of male teachers, because kindergarten and elementary school is taught primarily by females. The number of Kuwaiti female teachers,

**Table 4.1** *Number of students and teachers in public schools 1937-79*

| Year | Students Male | Female | Total | Teachers Male | Female | Total |
|------|------|--------|-------|------|--------|-------|
| 1937–8 | 620 | 140 | 760 | 30 | 5 | 35 |
| 1938–9 | 1,220 | 300 | 1,520 | 52 | 11 | 63 |
| 1939–40 | 1,500 | 330 | 1,830 | 58 | 11 | 69 |
| 1940–1 | 1,612 | 400 | 2,012 | 64 | 20 | 84 |
| 1941–2 | 1,700 | 460 | 2,160 | 67 | 22 | 89 |
| 1942–3 | 2,000 | 520 | 2,520 | 77 | 24 | 101 |
| 1943–4 | 2,300 | 590 | 2,890 | 84 | 27 | 111 |
| 1945–6 | 2,815 | 820 | 3,635 | 108 | 34 | 142 |
| 1946–7 | 3,027 | 935 | 3,962 | 126 | 37 | 163 |
| 1947–8 | 3,100 | 985 | 4,085 | 130 | 41 | 171 |
| 1948–9 | 3,450 | 1,215 | 4,665 | 150 | 48 | 198 |
| 1949–50 | 3,906 | 1,334 | 5,240 | 170 | 52 | 222 |
| 1950–1 | 4,520 | 1,772 | 6,292 | 212 | 82 | 294 |
| 1951–2 | 5,595 | 2,447 | 8,042 | 287 | 111 | 398 |
| 1952–3 | 7,188 | 3,550 | 10,738 | 394 | 170 | 564 |
| 1953–4 | 8,642 | 4,182 | 12,824 | 500 | 221 | 721 |
| 1954–5 | 10,100 | 5,200 | 15,300 | 630 | 291 | 921 |
| 1955–6 | 13,526 | 6,776 | 20,302 | 724 | 392 | 1,116 |
| 1956–7 | 15,946 | 8,578 | 24,524 | 882 | 543 | 1,425 |
| 1957–8 | 19,651 | 10,761 | 30,412 | 1,035 | 679 | 1,714 |
| 1958–9 | 21,764 | 12,661 | 34,425 | 1,092 | 750 | 1,842 |
| 1959–60 | 24,978 | 15,324 | 40,302 | 1,134 | 887 | 2,021 |
| 1960–1 | 27,698 | 17,459 | 45,157 | 1,248 | 1,007 | 2,255 |
| 1961–2 | 30,860 | 20,230 | 51,090 | 1,371 | 1,180 | 2,551 |
| 1962–3 | 35,674 | 23,877 | 59,551 | 1,551 | 1,390 | 2,941 |
| 1963–4 | 41,511 | 28,597 | 70,108 | 1,890 | 1,699 | 3,589 |
| 1964–5 | 46,613 | 32,506 | 79,119 | 2,241 | 1,914 | 4,155 |
| 1965–6 | 53,550 | 38,238 | 91,788 | 2,680 | 2,356 | 5,036 |
| 1966–7 | 58,702 | 43,026 | 101,728 | 2,967 | 2,701 | 5,668 |
| 1967–8 | 64,366 | 47,655 | 112,021 | 3,342 | 3,053 | 6,395 |
| 1968–9 | 68,877 | 51,673 | 120,550 | 3,811 | 3,506 | 7,317 |
| 1969–70 | 73,262 | 55,783 | 129,045 | 4,235 | 3,984 | 8,219 |
| 1970–1 | 78,363 | 60,384 | 138,747 | 4,639 | 4,446 | 9,085 |
| 1971–2 | 84,460 | 66,219 | 150,679 | 5,275 | 5,138 | 10,413 |
| 1972–3 | 88,897 | 71,334 | 160,231 | 5,734 | 5,771 | 11,505 |
| 1973–4 | 93,371 | 76,046 | 169,417 | 6,199 | 6,408 | 12,607 |
| 1974–5 | 100,061 | 82,717 | 182,778 | 6,990 | 7,223 | 14,213 |
| 1975–6 | 109,873 | 92,034 | 201,907 | 7,484 | 7,988 | 15,472 |
| 1976–7 | 127,380 | 107,823 | 235,203 | 8,862 | 9,360 | 18,222 |
| 1977–8 | 136,714 | 116,498 | 253,212 | 9,673 | 10,101 | 19,774 |
| 1978–9 | 143,586 | 123,932 | 267,518 | 10,158 | 10,466 | 20,624 |

Source: For 1937–77: Ministry of Education, *Annual Report 1968-9*; Ministry of Planning, *Annual Statistical Abstract 1976*, table 210; also Ministry of Education, Statistics Department, *General Census Report No. 2*, January 22, 1977; For 1977–9: Ministry of Planning, *Statistical Abstract 1979*, table 289, p. 331.

in fact, is almost double the number of male teachers. The 'female' role of teacher is accepted and encouraged by the transitional society of Kuwait.

Since the first school opened, education in Kuwait has been dependent on foreign manpower, primarily Arabs from Palestine and Egypt. The only time Kuwaiti teachers outnumbered other Arab teachers was prior to 1937. During 1976-7 the total number of non-Kuwaiti teachers was much higher than that of Kuwaiti teachers (table 4.2.)

**Table 4.2**  *Number of teachers, by nationality and sex*

| Nationality | Year | Male | Female | Total | % |
|---|---|---|---|---|---|
| Kuwaiti | 1976-7 | 1,824 | 3,205 | 5,029 | 27.7 |
| | 1977-8 | 1,975 | 3,332 | 5,307 | 26.8 |
| | 1978-9 | 2,109 | 3,396 | 5,505 | 26.7 |
| Egyptian | 1976-7 | 3,583 | 3,875 | 7,458 | 40.9 |
| | 1977-8 | 4,093 | 4,422 | 8,515 | 43.1 |
| | 1978-9 | 4,425 | 4,694 | 9,119 | 44.2 |
| Palestinian | 1976-7 | 2,983 | 1,860 | 4,843 | 26.6 |
| and | 1977-8 | 3,051 | 1,895 | 4,946 | 25.0 |
| Jordanian | 1978-9 | 3,074 | 1,910 | 4,984 | 24.2 |
| Syrian | 1976-7 | 272 | 109 | 381 | 2.6 |
| | 1977-8 | 333 | 202 | 535 | 2.7 |
| | 1978-9 | 331 | 190 | 521 | 2.5 |
| Iraqi | 1976-7 | 61 | 106 | 167 | 0.92 |
| | 1977-8 | 72 | 104 | 176 | 0.9 |
| | 1978-9 | 75 | 104 | 179 | 0.9 |
| Lebanese | 1976-7 | 48 | 38 | 86 | 0.47 |
| | 1977-8 | 47 | 34 | 81 | 0.4 |
| | 1978-9 | 44 | 37 | 81 | 0.4 |
| Other | 1976-7 | 91 | 113 | 204 | 1.1 |
| | 1977-8 | 96 | 118 | 214 | 1.1 |
| | 1978-9 | 100 | 135 | 235 | 1.1 |
| Total | 1976-7 | 8,862 | 9,306 | 18,168 | 100.0 |
| | 1977-8 | 9,667 | 10,107 | 19,774 | 100.0 |
| | 1978-9 | 10,158 | 10,466 | 20,624 | 100.0 |

Source: Ministry of Education, Statistics Department, *Census of Nationality of Male and Female Teachers*, 1976-7; Ministry of Planning, *Annual Statistical Abstract 1979*, table 298, p. 338, *Annual Statistical Abstract 1978*, table 297, p. 336.

The expansion of education at all levels has created an increasing demand for teachers and school staff. The salary is basically the same but the work is not as demanding and the chance of promotion is greater. To overcome this problem, the government now provides teachers with a bonus salary of 25 per cent above the basic salary.

The government provides free education for every child residing in Kuwait; this includes free books, school supplies, uniforms and meals. However, because of the large influx of foreigners during the last ten years, the government has limited admission to public schools. Priority is given to (1) children of Kuwaiti citizens; (2) children of the Gulf states, since education in the Gulf was introduced very recently; and (3) children from other Arab countries. The government maintains that not enough space exists to accommodate all the newcomers.

In 1975–6 some 80,663 non-Kuwaiti students attended public schools in Kuwait (table 4.3); another 32,020 attended Arabic-speaking private schools, and 14,362 attended foreign schools. Since 1970-1, the Ministry of Education has accepted between 5,000 and 6,000 immigrant children in the primary schools annually; however, during the academic year 1977-8, the public schools accepted 8,500 immigrant children in the elementary schools.[9] Most of the expatriate labor's children attend public schools.

The demand for education for migrant children has resulted in the opening of many private schools. From 3 schools in 1958, the number increased to a total of 83 by 1976. However, the problems of many Arab immigrants were not eliminated, particularly the Palestinians, who consistently demanded schools for their children. The government agreed to open the schools in the afternoon for Palestinian children who could not find a place in the morning school; the government paid all expenses for these children. The Ministry of Education and the PLO supervised the program. In 1976 the number of students in PLO schools was widely divided (table 4.4).

Since 1976 Palestinian females graduating from intermediate school have been accommodated into the government schools during the morning session. Table 4.4 does not include all Palestinian children; instead, only those who could not be placed in the morning schools are given.

Most students attending private schools are the children of expatriate labor whose parents incur considerable expense. The parents cannot usually therefore afford to pay for the education of their children. To alleviate this burden, the government began in 1975 to pay for half of the tuition of students enrolled in Arab private schools. Furthermore, it agreed to provide each student with all necessary textbooks free of charge, including KD10 ($35) towards each student's annual transport costs.[10]

**Table 4.3**  *Non-Kuwaiti students in public schools, by nationality and sex*

| Nationality | Year | Male | Female | Total |
|---|---|---|---|---|
| Palestinian | 1975-6 | 19,880 | 19,974 | 39,854 |
| and | 1976-7 | 31,477 | 29,891 | 61,368 |
| Jordanian | 1977-8 | 34,485 | 32,911 | 67,396 |
|  | 1978-9 | 37,332 | 35,502 | 72,834 |
| Egyptian |  | 2,281 | 2,317 | 4,598 |
|  |  | 2,674 | 2,665 | 5,339 |
|  |  | 3,218 | 3,163 | 6,381 |
|  |  | 3,658 | 3,447 | 7,105 |
| Syrian |  | 1,458 | 1,311 | 2,769 |
|  |  | 1,775 | 1,533 | 3,308 |
|  |  | 2,168 | 1,861 | 4,029 |
|  |  | 2,365 | 2,082 | 4,447 |
| Arabian Gulf | | 1,328 | 1,045 | 2,373 |
| States |  | 405 | 379 | 784 |
|  |  | 386 | 368 | 754 |
|  |  | 358 | 324 | 682 |
| Saudi Arabian |  | 2,035 | 1,625 | 3,660 |
|  |  | 2,101 | 1,783 | 3,884 |
|  |  | 2,242 | 1,874 | 4,116 |
|  |  | 2,227 | 1,955 | 4,182 |
| Iraqi |  | 1,981 | 1,735 | 3,716 |
|  |  | 2,214 | 2,001 | 4,215 |
|  |  | 2,386 | 2,265 | 4,651 |
|  |  | 2,523 | 2,351 | 4,874 |
| Lebanese |  | 1,608 | 1,555 | 3,163 |
|  |  | 1,812 | 1,828 | 3,640 |
|  |  | 1,960 | 1,942 | 3,902 |
|  |  | 2,128 | 2,144 | 4,272 |
| South Arabian |  | 1,098 | 563 | 1,661 |
|  |  | 1,870 | 1,229 | 3,099 |
|  |  | 1,793 | 1,264 | 3,057 |
|  |  | 2,091 | 1,634 | 3,725 |
| Other |  | 13,064 | 5,805 | 18,869 |
|  |  | 14,192 | 6,968 | 21,160 |
|  |  | 16,594 | 8,033 | 24,627 |
|  |  | 16,800 | 8,828 | 25,628 |
| Total | 75/76 | 44,733 | 35,930 | 80,663 |
|  | 76/77 | 58,520 | 48,277 | 106,797 |
|  | 77/78 | 65,232 | 53,681 | 118,913 |
|  | 78/79 | 69,482 | 58,267 | 127,749 |

Source: Ministry of Planning, *Annual Statistical Abstract 1976*, table 208; *Annual Statistical Abstract 1979*, table 297, p. 334.

**Table 4.4**     *Number of Palestinian schools, classrooms, teachers and students, 1976*

| Level of school | Schools | Classrooms | Teachers | Students |
|---|---|---|---|---|
| Primary: | | | | |
| Male | 6 | 66 | 99 | 1,796 |
| Female | 8 | 69 | 119 | 1,778 |
| Total | 14 | 135 | 218 | 3,574 |
| Intermediate: | | | | |
| Male | 9 | 172 | 338 | 5,196 |
| Female | 7 | 157 | 292 | 4,803 |
| Total | 16 | 329 | 630 | 9,999 |
| Secondary: | | | | |
| Male | 2 | 45 | 162 | 1,396 |
| Total: | | | | |
| Male | 17 | 283 | 599 | 8,388 |
| Female | 15 | 226 | 411 | 6,581 |
| Grand Total | 32 | 509 | 1,010 | 14,969 |

Source: Ministry of Planning, *Annual Statistical Abstract 1976*, table 220.

Traditionally, children of the elite in Kuwait attended public schools, while children of the foreign labor force attended private schools. During the past five years, however, some of the Kuwaiti elite have sent their children to various foreign private schools in the USA, Great Britain and France.

Currently, the Ministry of Education is confronted with a dilemma of quality versus quantity. If all the children of the migrant workers were accepted, the teacher-student ratio would be considerably decreased. Currently, this ratio is an acceptable 16.9 per cent in primary schools, 12.7 per cent in intermediate schools, and 9.2 per cent in secondary schools. Furthermore, admitting more students could compound the already overcrowded classroom situation: for 1978-9 the average student number per classroom for primary level was 30.8 for intermediate 29.8 and secondary 28.2 (table 4.5).[11]

Only since 1965 has compulsory education been introduced in Kuwait for all children between the ages of six and fourteen.[12] However, only 58 per cent of the eligible Kuwaitis are registered in school. The reasons for this lack of attendance among Kuwaiti children are numerous and complex, but one primary reason derives from the government's indecisiveness in implementing the compulsory education law. Nevertheless, the government is not entirely at fault — part of the problem lies in the laxity of many illiterate parents in sending their youngsters to school.

Another major problem is a high drop-out rate, which accounts for 0.6 per cent at elementary level, 6.1 per cent at intermediate level, and 8.65 per cent secondary level. In 1975, the Planning Board revealed that for every 1,000 Kuwaiti students who enter elementary school, only 52 students complete the secondary grades without failing courses during a twelve-year period.[13]

The cost of education varies from one level to the other. Table 4.6 shows the cost per annum.

## Higher education

The government of Kuwait considers highly qualified manpower to be one of the most important assets and many developed and under-developed countries, as well as Kuwait, are continually trying to increase their share of high-level manpower.

Prior to the opening of Kuwait University in 1966, secondary-school graduates were sent abroad at government expense, the particular university being determined by the student's area of study. During the early years of the program, most students preferred to study in one of Egypt's universities because the educational system in Cairo is comparable to that in Kuwait. Moreover, most students in the social sciences prefer to study their subjects in Arabic. Numerous Kuwaitis have graduated from other Arab countries, however, including the American University in Beirut, the University of Damascus and the University of Baghdad. Science students prefer to study in the USA, UK or France. In 1978 some 2,925 Kuwait students were studying in universities abroad (table 4.7).

Students studying at university abroad are usually sponsored by (1) one of the government ministries; (2) private sources, e.g. parents; or (3) an institution such as the Kuwait-Arab Planning Institute, Kuwait University, or one of the oil companies.

Kuwait University is supervised by the Ministry of Education and the University Council, which includes representatives from the private sector. The university began with the opening of five faculties in science, art and education, law and Sharia, commerce, and economics and political science. The schools of medicine and engineering opened in 1976. According to 1978 figures 67.1 per cent of the total student population attend Kuwait University.

Female Kuwaiti students at Kuwait University outnumber Kuwaiti male students; however, four times more males than females attend

**Table 4.5**  Number of government schools, classrooms, teachers and students, by sex and level of education 1977–8, 1978–9

| Year | Level of education | Schools | Classrooms | Teachers | Students | % students |
|------|-------------------|---------|------------|----------|----------|------------|
| 1977–8 | | | | | | |
| | *Kindergarten* | | | | | |
| | Male | Co-educational | | 1,196 | 7,992 | 51.9 |
| | Female | | | 1,196 | 7,420 | 48.1 |
| | Total | 56 | 646 | | 15,412 | 100.0 |
| | *Primary* | | | | | |
| | Male | 78 | 1,972 | 3,570 | 60,936 | 53.7 |
| | Female | 67 | 1,715 | 3,353 | 52,573 | 46.3 |
| | Total | 145 | 3,687 | 6,923 | 113,509 | 100.0 |
| | *Intermediate* | | | | | |
| | Male | 61 | 1,469 | 3,197 | 43,325 | 55.1 |
| | Female | 53 | 1,197 | 2,888 | 35,306 | 44.9 |
| | Total | 114 | 2,666 | 6,085 | 78,631 | 100.0 |
| | *Secondary* | | | | | |
| | Male | 29 | 722 | 2,107 | 20,605 | 52.0 |
| | Female | 27 | 674 | 2,247 | 19,030 | 48.0 |
| | Total | 56 | 1,396 | 4,354 | 39,635 | 100.0 |

1978-9

| | Co-educational | | | | |
|---|---|---|---|---|---|
| **Kindergarten** | | | | | |
| Male | | | | 8,349 | 51.5 |
| Female | | | | 7,850 | 48.5 |
| Total | 57 | 627 | 1,167 | 1,167 | 16,199 | 100.0 |
| **Primary** | | | | | |
| Male | 83 | 2,030 | 3,639 | 62,303 | 53.4 |
| Female | 71 | 1,755 | 3,279 | 54,418 | 46.6 |
| Total | 154 | 3,785 | 6,918 | 116,721 | 100.0 |
| **Intermediate** | | | | | |
| Male | 66 | 1,590 | 3,420 | 47,159 | 55.1 |
| Female | 56 | 1,282 | 3,048 | 38,430 | 44.9 |
| Total | 122 | 2,872 | 6,468 | 85,589 | 100.0 |
| **Secondary** | | | | | |
| Male | 33 | 778 | 2,317 | 22,180 | 51.5 |
| Female | 31 | 749 | 2,554 | 20,928 | 48.5 |
| Total | 64 | 1,527 | 4,871 | 43,108 | 100.0 |

Source: Ministry of Planning, *Annual Statistical Abstract 1979*, table 294, p. 334.

**Table 4.6**  *Cost per annum of each student in school, 1974-5*

| Level of Education | Cost (KD) |
| --- | --- |
| Kindergarten | 469 ($1,641) |
| Primary | 271 ($921) |
| Intermediate | 358 ($1,217) |
| Secondary | 498 ($1,693) |

Source: Ministry of Education, Information Department, February 1977.

universities abroad (table 4.8). Thus the role of women has not necessarily become more significant in Kuwait, even though they outnumber males at the University. Social barriers are the fundamental reason for the small number of females studying abroad (i.e., many conservative, traditional families absolutely refuse to allow their daughters to study abroad). Nevertheless, the Ministry of Education continues to encourage females to study in other Arab countries.

In terms of the area of academic specialization, females still choose those fields of study that are accepted by predominant social norms, i.e. medicine and social sciences. For example the number of females studying engineering, a traditionally male-orientated field, is extremely low: the percentage of female students studying engineering abroad is only 6.1 per cent; and the percentage in the engineering department at Kuwait University is only 8.9 per cent. Conversely, the percentage of Kuwait females studying art and education at Kuwait University is 79.2 per cent. Thus females in Kuwait still overwhelmingly choose to enter those fields traditionally reserved for women.

Highly skilled professionals are not only to be found at Kuwait University. In 1966 the Arab Planning Institute (previously called the Kuwait Institute of Economic and Social Planning in the Middle East) was established by the Government of Kuwait in accordance with the United Nations Development Program. The Institute's functions are: (1) to provide numerous training programs annually in various aspects of development planning for selected government and private-sector employees; (2) to conduct research activities related to economic, social and administrative aspects of planning; (3) to provide advisory services to the government; (4) to hold seminars for top-level government administrators and the private sector concerning improvement of administration; (5) to provide short courses (4–8 weeks) for government officials and other public organizations on various aspects of development planning and implementation. The institute provides diplomas to its trainees who attend the institute program for ten months. Until

**Table 4.7**  Students attending university abroad, by country and sex, 1978–9

| | Supported by Kuwait University * | | Supported by Ministry of Education + | | Self-supported + | | Supported by others + | | Total + | | General total | | Grand total |
|---|---|---|---|---|---|---|---|---|---|---|---|---|---|
| | m | f | m | f | m | f | m | f | m | f | m | f | |
| Egypt | 3 | 7 | 319 | 259 | 355 | 112 | 21 | 7 | 695 | 378 | 698 | 385 | 1,083 |
| Lebanon | – | – | – | 7 | 1 | 7 | – | 2 | 1 | 16 | 1 | 16 | 17 |
| Iraq | – | – | – | 1 | 2 | 1 | 13 | 13 | 15 | 15 | 15 | 15 | 30 |
| UK | 22 | 23 | 118 | 18 | 66 | 11 | 8 | 2 | 192 | 31 | 214 | 54 | 268 |
| USA | 130 | 30 | 624 | 17 | 405 | 17 | 136 | 8 | 1,165 | 42 | 1,295 | 72 | 1,367 |
| France | 6 | 1 | 5 | 35 | 2 | 2 | 6 | 4 | 13 | 41 | 19 | 42 | 61 |
| Pakistan | – | – | 3 | – | 2 | 2 | 5 | – | 10 | 2 | 10 | 2 | 12 |
| USSR | – | – | – | – | – | – | 20 | 1 | 20 | 1 | 20 | 1 | 21 |
| Other countries | 5 | 5 | 17 | 2 | 11 | 5 | 19 | 2 | 47 | 9 | 52 | 14 | 66 |
| Total | 166 | 66 | 1,086 | 339 | 844 | 157 | 228 | 39 | 2,158 | 535 | 2,324 | 601 | 2,925 |

* Postgraduate degrees
+ Undergraduate studies
Source: Ministry of Planning, *Annual Statistical Abstract 1979*.

**Table 4.8** *Number of Kuwait University students by field of study, sex and nationality, 1975–6*

| | Science | | Arts and education | | Law and Sharia | | Commerce, Economics, Political Science | | Engineering Petroleum | | Sum total | | Total |
|---|---|---|---|---|---|---|---|---|---|---|---|---|---|
| | m | f | m | f | m | f | m | f | m | f | m | f | |
| Kuwait | 184 | 327 | 259 | 986 | 117 | 77 | 389 | 394 | 62 | 6 | 1,011 | 1,790 | 2,801 |
| Gulf and Saudi Arabia | 114 | 50 | 94 | 317 | 31 | 10 | 162 | 122 | 9 | 4 | 410 | 503 | 913 |
| Foreign | 547 | 422 | 272 | 455 | 57 | 48 | 148 | 123 | 37 | 9 | 1,061 | 1,057 | 2,118 |
| Grand total | 845 | 799 | 625 | 1,758 | 205 | 135 | 699 | 639 | 108 | 19 | 2,482 | 3,350 | 5,832 |

Source: Kuwait University, Information and Secretariat Department, *Statistics for the Academic Year 1975–6.*

1973, the institute programs had been attended by 639 trainees, of whom 367 were officials of the Kuwaiti government and 272 from the Gulf and other Arab countries.[14]

## Problem of teachers

Kuwait, like many less developed countries, suffers from a shortage of teachers.[15] As a possible solution the Kuwaiti government has recruited many teachers from other Arab states. However, this has led to an extreme dependency by Kuwait on expatriate teachers, and to an especially heavy dependence on Egypt, where there is an excess of teachers.[16]

Although the Egyptian teachers teaching in Kuwait are well qualified, they use the traditional French models of education, which are now being abolished in France but which are still used in the Arab world.[17] Also the educational system in Egypt is designed to prepare people mainly for government service.[18] This system might be appropriate for Egypt with its large bureaucracy but it is not as applicable to a small country like Kuwait.

The hiring of teachers from other countries is expensive and especially so for Kuwait, since it provides its expatriate teachers and their dependents with such social services as education, health and sometimes housing.

It has not been possible to distribute more evenly the sources of expatriate teachers coming to Kuwait, mainly because other Arab countries in the region do not have a surplus of teachers. Nevertheless, Kuwait has managed to acquire teachers from a wide range of Arab countries (table 4.9).

To overcome the shortage of teachers, and to reverse the dependency on expatriate teachers, Kuwait strived for self-sufficiency by implementing teacher-training programs as early as 1951 and 1957. However, these programs failed, and in 1962 the Ministry of Education opened two teachers' institutes, one for males and one for females. Graduates of intermediate schools were accepted into the program. Students studied four years to become eligible for teaching at the primary-school level. In 1968, two teachers' training colleges were established. These colleges provided two years of training to secondary-school graduates, which allowed them to teach at the intermediate level. Then, in 1972–3 the old teachers' institutes were closed because graduates were not receiving sufficient training; moreover, during the same period a new teachers' training institute was opened, which required a secondary-school

**Table 4.9** *Number of teachers at all levels (except university), by sex and nationality, 1976–9*

| Year | Nationality | Male | Female | Total | % |
|---|---|---|---|---|---|
| 1976–7 | | | | | |
| | Kuwaiti | 1,824 | 3,205 | 5,029 | 27.5 |
| | Egyptian | 3,583 | 3,874 | 7,457 | 40.9 |
| | Jordanian and | | | | |
| | Palestinian | 2,983 | 1,860 | 4,843 | 26.5 |
| | Syrian | 272 | 169 | 441 | 2.5 |
| | Iraqi | 61 | 106 | 167 | 0.9 |
| | Lebanese | 48 | 38 | 86 | 0.5 |
| | Other | 91 | 113 | 204 | 1.2 |
| | Total | 8,862 | 9,365 | 18,227 | 100.0 |
| 1977–8 | | | | | |
| | Kuwaiti | 1,975 | 3,332 | 5,307 | 26.8 |
| | Egyptian | 4,093 | 4,422 | 8,515 | 43.1 |
| | Jordanian and | | | | |
| | Palestinian | 3,051 | 1,895 | 4,946 | 25.0 |
| | Syrian | 333 | 202 | 535 | 2.7 |
| | Iraqi | 72 | 104 | 176 | 0.9 |
| | Lebanese | 47 | 34 | 81 | 0.4 |
| | Other | 96 | 118 | 214 | 1.1 |
| | Total | 9,667 | 10,107 | 19,774 | 100.0 |
| 1978–9 | | | | | |
| | Kuwaiti | 2,109 | 3,396 | 5,505 | 26.7 |
| | Egyptian | 4,425 | 4,694 | 9,119 | 44.2 |
| | Jordanian and | | | | |
| | Palestinian | 3,074 | 1,910 | 4,984 | 24.2 |
| | Syrian | 331 | 190 | 521 | 2.5 |
| | Iraqi | 75 | 104 | 179 | 0.9 |
| | Lebanese | 44 | 37 | 81 | 0.4 |
| | Other | 100 | 135 | 235 | 1.1 |
| | Total | 10,158 | 10,466 | 20,624 | 100.0 |

*Source:* Ministry of Education; Statistics Department, *Statistics of the Number of Teachers by Nationality and Sex*, no. 12; *Annual Statistical Abstract 1978*, table 297, p. 336; *Annual Statistical Abstract 1979*, table 298, p. 338.

Note: The figures for 1976–7 do not include the administrative and clerical staff in the Ministry of Education. Furthermore, 2,394 additional employees are part of the ministry's staff; only 747 of these employees are Kuwaiti citizens.

certificate for admittance. This new teachers' training institute enrolled 367 males and 508 females, a relatively low total number of students.[19]

When Kuwaiti graduates returned from abroad and gradually became responsible members of the administration, they realized that the only way to improve the university was to change the old system and replace it with the American credit (units) system. Many of the older, more conservative, staff members were not prepared for the implementation of such a system; therefore, a program of re-education was adopted. Kuwait University started to recruit Arab-American graduates from the USA and other Arab graduates from American universities. Kuwait University sent students on scholarships to various foreign countries to pursue doctorates in many disciplines (table 4.10).

**Table 4.10** *Kuwait University MA and PhD scholarships, by country of destination, 1978–9*

| Country | Male | Female | Total |
| --- | --- | --- | --- |
| USA | 130 | 30 | 160 |
| UK | 22 | 23 | 45 |
| Egypt | 3 | 7 | 10 |
| Spain | 1 | 1 | 2 |
| France | 6 | 1 | 7 |
| Canada | 4 | – | 4 |
| Holland | – | 1 | 1 |
| Total | 166 | 63 | 229 |

Source: Kuwait University, Information and Secretariat Department, *Statistics Pamphlet 1978/9*.

The various government ministries also send their employees for training or for graduate and postgraduate programs abroad. In 1976, 632 civil employees were sent abroad by various ministries (this figure does not include the Ministry of Defense). The government has adopted a liberal policy towards its employees in that any employee who wants extensive training or further education is provided with a scholarship by the Civil Service; full pay would be provided at home and a student salary abroad. Such programs have been adopted in order to improve the caliber of employees.

## Vocational and technical education

Graduates from vocational and technical schools represent a small percentage of the total number of graduates from the various institutions in Kuwait. The vocational program is afflicted with major problems most of which derive from the pejorative stereotype that continues to be associated with manual work. The government has attempted to change this attitude by introducing various vocational programs.

This first school for the Vocational Training of Labor was established by the Ministry of Social Affairs and Labor. The principal objectives of this type of school were: (1) to improve the skills and the general conditions of the labor force so that eventually it would be able to compete with the foreign labor force in the market; and (2) to satisfy current and future manpower requirements.

In 1955, the first year of the program, there were 1,773 applicants; only 107 were accepted. Because the government had insufficient facilities for such a large number of applicants, enrollment was limited to those people who were able to read and write.[20] The classes were conducted at night and the government provided financial assistance and other aid to those attending. Table 4.11 shows how they divided into various fields of study.

**Table 4.11**    *School for Vocational Training of Labor: numbers enlisted and specialization, 1955-8*

| Field of specialization | Number enlisted | | | |
|---|---|---|---|---|
| | *1955* | *1956* | *1957* | *1958* |
| Electrician | 30 | 20 | 26 | 25 |
| Carpenter (workshop) | 8 | – | – | – |
| Welder | 8 | 7 | 13 | 10 |
| Plumber | 13 | 17 | 16 | 8 |
| Metal lather | 12 | 31 | 18 | 19 |
| Furniture craftsman | 19 | 28 | 31 | 22 |
| Automechanic | 17 | 36 | 40 | 21 |
| Foundry | – | 12 | 17 | 4 |
| Fitter | – | 3 | 23 | 8 |
| Upholsterer | – | – | 5 | 8 |
| Total | 107 | 154 | 189 | 125 |

Source: Ministry of Social Affairs and Labor, Annual Report 1958, p. 25.

The Ministry of Education established the Industrial College in 1954 for students who had graduated from intermediate school and had decided not to continue their high-school education. This school offered four-year programs in such diverse fields as auto-mechanics, telecommunications, electronics, carpentry and industrial design. Despite the ministry's assistance, such as providing students with a monthly salary of KD30 ($105), in addition to free room and board, attendance was very low. In 1956-7, for example, only 98 students enrolled, even though the school's capacity was 600 students. Table

**Table 4.12**   *Industrial College – number of graduates, 1957–74*

| Academic year | Number of graduates |
|---|---|
| 1957–8 | 7 |
| 1958–9 | 33 |
| 1959–60 | 29 |
| 1960–1 | 35 |
| 1961–2 | 47 |
| 1962–3 | 26 |
| 1963–4 | 33 |
| 1964–5 | 56 |
| 1965–6 | 67 |
| 1966–7 | 23 |
| 1967–8 | 36 |
| 1968–9 | 71 |
| 1969–70 | 120 |
| 1970–1 | 139 |
| 1971–2 | 108 |
| 1972–3 | 146 |
| 1973–4 | 164 |
| Total | 1,140 |

Source: J. A. Socknat, 'An Inventory and Assessment of Employment-Oriented Human Resources Development Program in the Gulf Area,' Bahrain Conference on Human Resources in the Gulf, February 1975.

4.12 shows the number of graduates during the period 1957-74.

In 1952 the Ministry of Education also opened the Commercial School, which was designed for government employees and individuals in the private sector interested in learning a trade. The primary courses offered were English, Arabic, typing, and accounting. Overall employee enrollment in the Commercial School was considerably higher than in the Industrial College. When the school first opened in 1952 it had twelve students; however, by 1955 total enrollment had increased to 364 students.[21]

As vocational training expanded rapidly, organized training units began to increase. By 1974-5, more than ten training units were established in addition to those of the ministries. They were divided into groups with organized training and were implemented through an organized institution, each of which had an independent budget and a full-time faculty in both theoretical and applied sciences (table 4.13).

The vocational training program in the government sector was implemented through the various ministries but was carried out without any co-ordinated plan. For example, each ministry initiated and administered its own vocational education program without any determination of the actual educational needs of the country overall. The

**Table 4.13** *Organized training by ministry, number of students and required certificate, 1973*

| Institute | Year established | Required school certificate | Duration of study (years) | Student enrollment | Ministry responsible |
|---|---|---|---|---|---|
| Agriculture Institute | 1969 | Secondary | 2 | 22 | Public Work |
| Civil Aviation | 1969 | Secondary | 1–2 | 25 | Defense |
| Fire Brigade School | 1967 | Intermediate | 1⅓ | 80 | Municipality |
| Shawikh Training Center | 1967 | Secondary | 1 | 186 | Social Affairs and Labor |
| Institute for Applied Engineering | 1968 | Secondary | 2 | 57 | Public Work |
| Institute of Nursing (all female) | 1962 | Intermediate | 3 | 150 | Health |
| Telecommunication | 1966 | Intermediate | 2 | 354 | Communication |
| Water Resources Center | 1968 | Intermediate | 1½ | 96 | Electricity and Water |
| Health Occupations and Training | 1974/5 | Secondary | 2 | 129 (female) | Health |
| Vocational and Technical Education for Females | 1963 | Intermediate | 4 | 440 | Social Affairs and Labor |

Source: Council of Ministers Central Vocational Training Directorate 'Assessment of the Training Potentials in the Government Sector' (Arabic), April 1973; Socknat, *op. cit.*

Planning Board (Ministry of Planning) conducted a study of various vocational training programs and in 1972 recommended the establishment of a new agency: the Central Vocational Training Directorate. The main objective was to improve, co-ordinate, and evaluate the activities of the various institutes within a period of three years. Essentially, it prepared the groundwork for government improvement and centralization of the various training programs.

The number of students attending the Industrial College and various vocational programs is relatively low. This is due to numerous social and cultural factors. Many people in less developed countries such as Kuwait believe manual workers are inferior members of the work force; thus white-collar workers are frequently given a higher status. The reason for this widespread belief derives from the Bedouin dislike of a settled life as perceived through the peasant who uses his hands.[22] Furthermore, many students prefer to continue their general education because they realize that they will achieve higher status if they are graduates of a university or college as opposed to an industrial college. Under the Civil Service salary scale, a graduate from a university or college receives a higher salary (fourth grade) than a graduate from an industrial college (sixth grade). Finally, many students who enlist in the vocational training programs are students who have failed to make it in school and they enlist themselves on a temporary basis until they find other available employment in the government or the private sector. While searching for suitable employment, these students live on wages from the government by going to vocational schools and then drop out as soon as they find a job; this is substantiated by the percentage of vocational training drop outs, which reached 39 per cent during 1970–1.[23]

### On-the-job training

On-the-job training is financed by the ministry concerned and does not have an independent budget. The trainees receive practical training only because there are no theoretical courses such as those a co-ordinated plan might contain. Most of the people who become involved in such a program are unemployed Kuwaitis who want to learn a skill. The basic program is divided between the various ministries as shown in table 4.14.

The level of the graduates varies from one center to another, depending on the student's period of enrollment (six months, one year, or two years) and the particular program of training. The graduates are

**Table 4.14**  *Job training, 1972*

| Type | Ministry | No. of students |
|---|---|---|
| Inspector training | Public Works | 11 |
| Wasem (trade and business auditor) | Trade and Industry | 19 |
| Health training center | Health | 35 |
| Information | Information | – |

Source: Council of Ministers Central Vocational Training Directorate, *op. cit.*, p. 4.

classified according to three levels: (1) semi-skilled worker; (2) skilled worker; and (3) technician.

### The cost of vocational and technical education

The cost of vocational and technical education is extremely high; it varies from one institute or center to the other, as shown in table 4.15.

There are several problems associated with the high cost of vocational and technical education, particularly at the secondary level. Modernizing countries often waste large sums of money in misplaced emphasis on primary and secondary vocational schools. In some countries, for example, students who prove to be unfit for higher academic training are sent to vocational schools, and as a consequence these institutions become the catchbasins for incompetents, and in many instances the training they receive tends to be of poor quality and not specifically related to the occupations which the students later enter.[24] Furthermore, to hire a competent technical staff requires a substantial financial investment; most are expatriates, who demand higher wages and benefits, and they consequently bring high social-overhead costs compared to nationals.[25]

**Table 4.15**  *Cost of vocational and educational training (KD)*

| Institute | Cost per trainee |
|---|---|
| Agricultural Institute | 4,384 ($15,344) |
| Institute of Applied Engineering | 2,866 ($10,031) |
| Wireless and Telecommunication Center | 4,388 ($15,358) |
| Water Resources Development Center | 400 ($1,400) |
| Air Aviation Training Center | 1,466 ($5,131) |
| Shawikh Vocational Training | 1,145 ($4,075) |

Source: Council of Ministers Central Vocational Training Directorate, *op. cit.*, p. 12.

Are the extremely high costs of vocational and technical education in Kuwait justified? Statistics reveal that many trainees end up in job positions that do not relate to the type of training received.[26] In 1974, the Ministry of Social Affairs and Labor conducted an empirical study to follow up on graduates of vocational training; the study showed that 49.2 per cent of the graduates who were originally trained in vocational and technical institutions neither accepted nor preferred manual work. Furthermore, this study revealed that 87 per cent of the graduates of wireless and communications rejected manual labor even though their training was essentially manual. Finally, the report showed that 86 per cent of the graduates who did work in their field of specialization required re-training before they were employed.[27]

### Vocational training in the private sector

After the government, the private sector is the largest employer in the state; therefore, its role in the field of vocational training has been significant. According to a 1973 survey, there were 104,679 employees in the private sector; the number of establishments was 19,357. The number of Kuwaitis in this sector was relatively small, totaling 7,830 people — which included employers, administrators, and workers. The number of Kuwaitis in this sector accounted for only 7.5 per cent. This low percentage was largely due to the general reluctance by many Kuwaitis to accept positions in the private sector because it does not provide Social-security benefits. However, this situation was rectified in 1977 by the formation of the Kuwait Social Security system, which includes both the government and the private sectors. Another reason why many Kuwaitis refuse to work in the private sector is that many companies require their employees to work longer hours.

The distribution of labor by occupation in the private sector reveals certain trends in the position of Kuwaiti workers (table 4.16). Based on these figures, opportunities exist for young Kuwaitis to join this sector if they are given the appropriate training.

As in the government sector, in terms of actual training programs there is no co-ordination between the various companies, with each company having its own independent training program. These programs are usually on-the-job training; however, certain companies send their employees abroad for further study or specialization. For example, Prefabricated Houses sends some employees to Sweden; and Kuwait Navigation Company sends many of its employees to the USSR and Egypt. Two joint-sector companies have their own training centers:

Table 4.16  Relative distribution of workers by occupation in six companies

| Company | Top management | | | Technicians | | | Skilled workers | | | Clerical | | | Total | % Kuwaitis |
|---|---|---|---|---|---|---|---|---|---|---|---|---|---|---|
| | K | nK | K% | K | nK | K% | K | nK | K% | K | nK | K% | | |
| Cement Co. | 2 | 11 | 15 | 4 | 6 | 40 | – | 70 | 0 | 4 | 15 | 21 | 112 | 8.9 |
| Fish Co. | 5 | 14 | 26 | – | 113 | 0 | – | 160 | 0 | 50 | – | 100 | 342 | 16.9 |
| Pipes Co. | 3 | 22 | 12 | – | 3 | 0 | – | 130 | 0 | – | 12 | 0 | 170 | 1.76 |
| Pre-Fab Co. | 8 | 30 | 21 | – | 61 | 0 | – | 11 | 0 | 2 | 25 | 6.8 | 137 | 7.2 |
| Chemical Co. | 11 | 118 | 8.5 | 5 | 372 | 1.3 | 33 | 400 | 7.6 | 6 | 119 | 4.8 | 1,064 | 5.1 |
| Flour Mills | 5 | 19 | 20 | 3 | 60 | 4.7 | – | 162 | – | 10 | 263 | 3.6 | 522 | 3.4 |
| Total | 34 | 214 | | 12 | 615 | | 33 | 933 | | 72 | 434 | | 2,347 | 6.4 |

Source: M. A. El Kalyoub, *Manpower Development in Kuwait*, Arab Planning Institute, Kuwait, 1974.

Kuwait Chemical Fertilizer Company, and the Kuwait National Petro-leum Company. These two companies provide training for their own workers, as well as occasionally for employees from other companies.

## Vocational training in the oil sector

The following five foreign oil companies and one national oil company currently operate in Kuwait:

(1) Kuwait Oil Company: formed in 1934 and the largest oil com-pany operating in Kuwait; it is jointly owned by British Petroleum and Gulf Oil Company.

(2) American Independent Oil Company: began its operations in the neutral zone between Kuwait and Saudi Arabia in 1948.

(3) Arabian Oil Company: began its operations in 1959; this Japanese company operates in the off-shore area of Kuwait and Saudi Arabia.

(4) Kuwait Spanish Oil Company: started its operation in 1969.

(5) Kuwait Shell Oil Company: began its operations in 1961; it is owned by Shell and operates in the off-shore area of Kuwait.

(6) Kuwait National Petroleum Company: founded in 1960, it is the only national company.

Employment in the oil companies varies widely (table 4.17). As with other sectors of the economy, Kuwaitis constitute a relatively low percentage of employees in the oil sector, which is considered the back-bone of the Kuwaiti economy. Furthermore, the number of Kuwaitis employed in this sector has not increased considerably but the number of Arabs has and the number of foreigners has declined significantly. The primary reason for the relatively low number of Kuwaitis employed in the oil sector is that even though the wages offered by the oil com-panies are similar to those of the government, the oil companies do not provide social-security and retirement benefits. Also, the oil fields are located around the city of Ahmadi, which is thirty miles outside Kuwait City, which could be another reason for the Kuwaitis' reluctance since most of them own homes near Kuwait City and it would obviously be an inconvenience to commute thirty miles daily, particularly during the summer when the temperature generally averages more than 100 degrees. Furthermore, although the oil companies provide housing for their employees in the city of Ahmadi, most Kuwaitis insist on staying near Kuwait City.

**Table 4.17**   *Employment in the oil companies, 1961, 1971*

| Company | 1961 | % | 1971 | % |
|---|---|---|---|---|
| | | Number of employees | | |
| **(1)  Kuwait Oil Co.** | | | | |
| Kuwaitis | 1,424 | 23.4 | 1,434 | 43.48 |
| Arabs | 1,659 | 27.2 | 1,221 | 37.02 |
| Foreigners | 3,006 | 49.4 | 643 | 19.5 |
| Total | 6,089 | 100.0 | 3,298 | 100.0 |
| **(2)  American Independent** | | | | |
| Kuwaitis | 5 | 0.81 | 102 | 4.86 |
| Arabs | 302 | 48.95 | 1,013 | 48.31 |
| Foreigners | 310 | 50.24 | 982 | 46.83 |
| Total | 617 | 100.0 | 2,097 | 100.0 |
| **(3)  Arabian Oil Co.*** | | | | |
| Kuwaitis | 1 | 0.25 | 101* | 7.66 |
| Arabs | 205 | 52 | 1,058 | 80.27 |
| Foreigners | 188 | 47.75 | 159 | 12.06 |
| Total | 394 | 100.0 | 1,318 | 100.0 |
| **(4)  Kuwait National Petrol** | | | | |
| Kuwaitis | 6 | 0.72 | 261 | 15.25 |
| Arabs | 216 | 90.76 | 1,198 | 69.98 |
| Foreigners | 16 | 6.7 | 253 | 14.78 |
| Total | 238 | 100.0 | 1,712 | 100.0 |
| **(5)  Spanish Oil** | | | | |
| Kuwaitis | – | – | 13 | 39.4 |
| Arabs | – | – | 13 | 39.4 |
| Foreigners | – | – | 7 | 21.2 |
| Total | – | – | 33 | 100.0 |
| **Grand Total:** | | | | |
| Kuwaitis | 1,436 | 19.6 | 1,911 | 22.6 |
| Arabs | 2,382 | 32.5 | 4,503 | 53.2 |
| Foreigners | 3,520 | 47.9 | 2,044 | 24.2 |
| Total | 7,338 | 100.0 | 8,458 | 100.0 |

* Arabian Oil Co. figures are for 1970 not 1971.
Source: L. Saraff, *Training Programs for Manpower Development in the Oil Companies in Kuwait*, Arab Planning Institute, Kuwait, 1972.

The employment level at Kuwait Oil Company has declined largely because KOC had finished with the exploration stage, which also explains the decline in the number of foreigners. The foreign labor force consisted of British, Americans, Indians and Pakistanis – either highly qualified workers or skilled laborers. In the initial stage of exploration, these foreigners were in high demand; however, after Kuwait's independence in 1961 and the government's insistence that more Kuwaitis and Arabs be employed, the percentage of foreigners declined, from 47.9 per cent in 1961 to 24.2 per cent in 1971.

## Distribution by occupation

Table 4.18 shows the distribution of the labor force by occupation in the oil companies. This distribution shows the type of training that is needed. Kuwaitis are employed in two major branches of the oil industry: crude oil and natural gas; and oil refining:. In 1970, the total number of Kuwaitis employed in these two branches was 1,741 – or 96.83 per cent of the total Kuwaiti labor force. The reason for this concentration in these branches of the oil industry is that they require little education and pay relatively well.

## Vocational training

The oil companies in Kuwait were the first to recognize and stress the importance of vocational education. In 1945, Kuwait Oil Company opened the first vocational training center to improve the quality of the Kuwaiti labor force by offering extensive training programs. Different levels of training are presently available in the company, such as workers' training, medium-level training, and high-level on-the-job training.

As indicated, most of the oil companies maintain on-the-job training programs. Training courses are available to company employees, which concentrates in the fields of administration, technical work and foreign language (English). During the 1964–70 period,[28] the foreign oil companies sent 40 employees out of a total of 6,746 for specialized training in the USA and the UK. This is a relatively low number compared to that of Kuwait National Petroleum Company (KNPC), which during this same period sent 37 students or employees abroad out of a total of only 1,712.

## Summary

The expansion of the educational system in Kuwait over the last thirty years has been one of the most visible and significant aspects of social development in the country. The demand for education for their children by both native Kuwaitis and immigrants has been the primary reason for this expansion. For example, the number of expatriate children attending school in Kuwait (government and private) rose

**Table 4.18** *Distribution of employees according to occupation, (12 years and more), 1970*

| Section of economic activities | Total | Section of main professions | | | | | | | | Total |
|---|---|---|---|---|---|---|---|---|---|---|
| | | Professional & technical | Management & administration | Clerical | Sales | Services | Agriculture | Production | Not stated | |
| Crude oil and natural gas | K | 74 | 15 | 194 | 6 | 176 | 3 | 1,030 | 6 | 1,504 |
| | nK | 743 | 101 | 859 | 17 | 356 | 25 | 1,799 | 5 | 3,905 |
| | Total | 817 | 116 | 1,053 | 23 | 532 | 28 | 2,829 | 11 | 5,409 |
| Operations and research | K | 1 | 1 | 2 | 1 | 1 | — | 12 | — | 18 |
| | nK | 56 | 4 | 23 | 2 | 15 | — | 88 | — | 188 |
| | Total | 57 | 5 | 25 | 3 | 16 | — | 100 | — | 206 |
| Other activities | K | — | — | 1 | — | 1 | — | 10 | — | 12 |
| | nK | 23 | 3 | 6 | 1 | — | — | 86 | — | 119 |
| | Total | 23 | 3 | 7 | 1 | 1 | — | 96 | — | 131 |
| Oil refining | K | 34 | 2 | 37 | — | 16 | 1 | 182 | 1 | 273 |
| | nK | 458 | 8 | 198 | 8 | 64 | 3 | 158 | — | 897 |
| | Total | 492 | 10 | 235 | 8 | 80 | 4 | 340 | 1 | 1,170 |
| Cement and tar manufacturing | K | 1 | 1 | 3 | — | 1 | — | 11 | — | 17 |
| | nK | 6 | — | 3 | — | 1 | — | 47 | — | 57 |
| | Total | 7 | 1 | 6 | — | 2 | — | 58 | — | 74 |
| Bottled gas | K | — | 1 | 1 | — | — | — | 10 | — | 10 |
| | nK | — | 1 | 1 | — | 3 | — | 66 | — | 71 |
| | Total | — | 1 | 1 | — | 3 | — | 76 | — | 81 |
| Other industry with oil and coal | K | — | — | — | — | — | — | — | — | |
| | nK | 13 | — | — | — | 1 | — | — | — | 14 |
| | Total | 13 | — | — | — | 1 | — | — | — | 14 |

Source: El Kalyoub, *op. cit.*

from 75,305 in 1970-1 to 115,268 students in 1974-5; moreover, their percentage among the entire student population increased from 43 per cent to 50 per cent during the same period. This increased demand for education necessitated some schools in Kuwait to operate 'full time,' or in three shifts: the morning period, which held regular classes; the afternoon period, attended by PLO schools; and the evening classes, used for adult-education programs.

Despite government efforts in the field of education, the number of illiterates in the population is still high (table 4.19). The primary reasons for this derive from the naturalization of the Arab nomad, Badu (see chapter 5 for details). Since a substantial percentage of Kuwaiti adults is illiterate – particularly among these nomad migrants – considerable emphasis recently has been on adult education.

Although vocational and adult education recently has been emphasized in Kuwait, the priority is still general, formalized education (table 4.20). Consequently, more graduates will have high-level professional skills; but their percentage will remain low (table 4.1). Nevertheless, future university graduates increasingly will enter many highly responsible positions.

The real shortage in the future will be in such middle-level occupations as technicians and skilled laborers. In response to this developing problem the government has established many vocational schools and centers; however, constructing the facilities at an increasing rate does not ensure that there will be enough graduates from these vocational schools.[29] A definite need exists to focus more on the educational system as a whole. One cannot change people's behavior and attitudes through building more schools and vocational centers – one must start with changing people's attitudes. The current experiment with vocational education in Kuwait has proved to be a costly failure. As described, many students who enter vocational programs are drop-outs from regular schools; others enter vocational schools because the government provides them with such incentives as an attractive salary.

A similarity exists between young Kuwaitis and the youth of other less developed countries; from their perspective, education is a passport to the government's bureaucratic hierarchy. The government is partially responsible for this trend because its employment policy gives young graduates such preferential treatment as 'fourth-grade' salary, regardless of their degree. As stated, this experience is not unique to Kuwait; it applies to the Third World in general:[30]

> In almost all nations of Africa, Asia, and Latin America, entry into
> modern sector public and private jobs is predicated upon successful

**Table 4.19**  Illiterate population, census years 1957, 1961, 1965, 1970, 1975

| Years | Sex | Population | | | No. illiterates | | | % illiterates | | |
|---|---|---|---|---|---|---|---|---|---|---|
| | | K | nK | Total | K | nK | Total | K | nK | Total |
| 1957 | M | 38,461 | 61,669 | 100,130 | 17,834 | 30,722 | 48,556 | 46.4 | 49.8 | 48.5 |
| | F | 35,287 | 12,123 | 47,410 | 26,168 | 5,757 | 31,925 | 74.2 | 47.5 | 67.3 |
| | T | 73,748 | 73,792 | 147,540 | 44,002 | 36,479 | 80,481 | 59.7 | 49.4 | 54.6 |
| 1961 | M | 59,969 | 100,498 | 160,467 | 22,636 | 43,173 | 65,809 | 37.7 | 43.0 | 41.0 |
| | F | 54,190 | 30,430 | 84,620 | 33,005 | 12,819 | 45,824 | 60.9 | 42.1 | 54.2 |
| | T | 114,159 | 130,928 | 245,087 | 55,641 | 55,992 | 111,633 | 48.8 | 42.8 | 45.6 |
| 1965 | M | 70,859 | 144,391 | 215,250 | 27,925 | 56,791 | 84,716 | 39.4 | 39.3 | 39.4 |
| | F | 67,169 | 45,265 | 112,434 | 46,678 | 18,159 | 64,837 | 60.5 | 40.1 | 57.7 |
| | T | 138,028 | 189,656 | 327,684 | 74,603 | 74,950 | 149,553 | 54.0 | 39.5 | 45.6 |
| 1970 | M | 110,846 | 184,207 | 295,053 | 35,519 | 58,717 | 94,236 | 32.0 | 31.9 | 31.5 |
| | F | 108,246 | 89,532 | 197,778 | 67,858 | 31,177 | 99,035 | 62.7 | 34.8 | 50.1 |
| | T | 219,092 | 273,739 | 492,831 | 103,377 | 89,894 | 193,271 | 47.2 | 32.8 | 39.0 |
| 1975 | M | 149,654 | 225,403 | 375,057 | 44,880 | 61,889 | 106,769 | 30.0 | 27.5 | 28.5 |
| | F | 150,120 | 137,219 | 287,339 | 88,734 | 42,971 | 131,705 | 59.1 | 31.3 | 45.8 |
| | T | 299,774 | 362,622 | 662,396 | 133,614 | 104,860 | 238,474 | 44.6 | 28.9 | 36.0 |

Note: Data for 1957, 1965, 1970 and 1975 refer to population 10 years of age and more. Data for 1961 refer to persons 6 years of age and more.

Source: Ministry of Planning, *Annual Statistical Abstract 1976*.

**Table 4.20** Total enrollment in adult-education programs, 1976–9

| Year | Sex | Secondary | | Intermediate | | Eradication of Illiterates | | Classrooms | | | Total | | |
|---|---|---|---|---|---|---|---|---|---|---|---|---|---|
| | | non-Kuwaiti | Kuwaiti | non-Kuwaiti | Kuwaiti | non-Kuwaiti | Kuwaiti | Secondary | Inter-mediate | Eradication of illiterates | No. of centers | non-Kuwaiti | Kuwaiti |
| 1976–7 | M | 2,064 | 2,423 | 3,560 | 2,138 | 3,551 | 865 | 162 | 234 | 181 | 78 | 9,175 | 5,426 |
| | F | 800 | 1,235 | 1,333 | 1,222 | 1,161 | 953 | 85 | 135 | 93 | 60 | 3,294 | 3,410 |
| | T | 2,864 | 3,658 | 4,893 | 3,360 | 4,712 | 1,818 | 247 | 369 | 274 | 138 | 12,469 | 8,836 |
| 1977–8 | M | 1,930 | 2,613 | 2,738 | 2,141 | 2,174 | 544 | 157 | 198 | 111 | 73 | 6,842 | 5,298 |
| | F | 684 | 1,235 | 1,102 | 1,205 | 597 | 845 | 82 | 123 | 80 | 60 | 2,383 | 3,285 |
| | T | 2,614 | 3,848 | 3,840 | 3,346 | 2,771 | 1,389 | 239 | 321 | 191 | 133 | 9,225 | 8,583 |
| 1978–9 | M | 1,921 | 3,174 | 2,575 | 2,597 | 2,029 | 625 | 153 | 177 | 90 | 75 | 6,525 | 6,396 |
| | F | 665 | 1,366 | 838 | 1,295 | 298 | 931 | 80 | 120 | 65 | 65 | 1,801 | 3,592 |
| | T | 2,586 | 4,540 | 3,413 | 3,892 | 2,327 | 1,556 | 233 | 297 | 155 | 140 | 8,326 | 9,988 |

Source: Ministry of Planning, Annual Statistical Abstract 1979, table 312, p. 355.

**Table 4.21** *College graduates for academic years, 1974–80** *

| Academic year | Kuwait University | | Universities Abroad | | Teachers' College | | Total | |
|---|---|---|---|---|---|---|---|---|
| | *m* | *f* | *m* | *f* | *m* | *f* | *m* | *f* |
| 1974–75 | 126 | 248 | 90 | 15 | 60 | 319 | 276 | 582 |
| 1975–6 | 143 | 324 | 90 | 15 | 67 | 350 | 300 | 689 |
| 1976–7 | 166 | 414 | 80 | 14 | 74 | 412 | 320 | 840 |
| 1977–8 | 174 | 523 | 80 | 14 | 82 | 489 | 336 | 1,026 |
| 1978–9 | 194 | 624 | 70 | 12 | 92 | 532 | 356 | 1,168 |
| 1979–80 | 212 | 740 | 70 | 12 | 102 | 557 | 384 | 1,309 |
| Total | 1,015 | 2,873 | 480 | 82 | 477 | 2,659 | 1,972 | 5,614 |

* Figures include Kuwaiti and non-Kuwaiti graduates.
Source: Five-Year Development Plan.

completion of the requisite years of education associated with particular jobs, often irrespective of whether or not such education requirements are really necessary for satisfactory job performance.

The improvement of the educational system in Kuwait should not mean school expansion and increased enrollment; instead, the 'methods' or 'philosophy' must be changed. The success of the educational system in Kuwait largely depends on its ability to adapt to the country's changing environment in particular, and the rapidly changing world in general.

Chapter 5

# Toward manpower planning
# in Kuwait

Throughout this study the manpower situation in Kuwait has been described to have the following characteristics:

(1)   There is a severe shortage in the Kuwaiti labor force at all levels (i.e., professional, technical and unskilled labor). This shortage was a result of the rapid expansion and growth of the Kuwaiti economy: a high demand for labor was created which the native Kuwaiti population was unable to meet, and as a consequence the majority of jobs were filled by an expatriate labor force.

(2)   The young age of the Kuwaiti population, combined with a low participation rate of Kuwaiti women and a high illiteracy rate among the Kuwaiti labor force, are important contributing factors to the manpower problem in Kuwait (see table 2.3).

(3)   The concentration of the majority of the Kuwaiti labor force in the service sector (government) along with the refusal to take on any type of technical or manual work has contributed to the shortage of Kuwaiti employees in the national labor force.

This chapter will propose a plan which in the light of the availability of manpower, or the lack thereof, will reflect the reality of the present situation. One should keep in mind, however, that it is not intended to provide an estimate of manpower requirements for the country, for this is dependent upon Kuwait's economic goals, which are still being defined.

A better and more efficient utilization of the existing manpower situation in Kuwait will be proposed, one which can be achieved mainly through the restructuring of the existing system of employment. Political, social and economic components exist which are vital to the success of manpower development and planning in Kuwait. There is a need to improve labor productivity in the government sector. This in turn requires measures related to the reduction and improvement of the quality of public-sector employees. Future generations to be employed in the labor force must be adequately prepared from the standpoint of general, technical and vocational education. The female population in the country needs to be encouraged to participate more widely in the labor force, and actions to this end should begin in the earliest stages of the educational process. Furthermore, taking into consideration the small size of Kuwait and its limited population it is of utmost importance to reform the naturalization and immigration laws.

## Reforming the civil service

The welfare philosophy of the State of Kuwait has resulted in an extremely large number of civil-service employees — 124,781 out of a total population of 994,837 and a labor force of 304,600. This means that 41 per cent of the entire labor force is employed in the government sector.

Two of the key problems of the civil service are widespread illiteracy and overstaffed and under-utilized personnel. The *number* of well qualified civil servants is very low. This is well illustrated in table 5.1.

**Table 5.1**  *Government civil servants, by educational attainment, 1976*

| Educational attainment | Kuwaitis | | non-Kuwaitis | | Total | |
|---|---|---|---|---|---|---|
| | No. | % | No. | % | No. | % |
| Illiterate | 11,265 | 24.1 | 18,717 | 26.2 | 29,982 | 25.7 |
| Read and write | 14,642 | 31.3 | 19,817 | 28.5 | 34,459 | 29.6 |
| Primary | 3,778 | 8.1 | 2,674 | 3.8 | 6,452 | 5.5 |
| Intermediate | 6,217 | 13.3 | 3,301 | 4.7 | 9,518 | 8.2 |
| Secondary | 6,067 | 13.0 | 10,472 | 15.0 | 16,539 | 14.2 |
| Below university level | 1,761 | 3.8 | 1,683 | 2.4 | 3,444 | 3.0 |
| First university degree | 2,875 | 6.1 | 12,099 | 17.4 | 14,974 | 12.9 |
| Postgraduate | 164 | 0.3 | 919 | 1.3 | 1,083 | 0.9 |
| Total | 46,769 | 100.0 | 69,682 | 100.0 | 116,451 | 100.0 |

Source: Ministry of Planning, *Annual Statistical Abstract 1979*, table 129, p. 137.

Table 5.1 indicates that 25 per cent of civil-service employees are illiterate, a fact which undoubtedly affects the performance and productivity of the entire civil service in that the presence of illiterate and untrained employees inevitably results in a decline in man-hour output. The few qualified civil-service administrators are unable to perform their jobs adequately because of the illiteracy of the lower-level employees.

The absence of middle-level manpower has undoubtedly handicapped the development of an adequate and efficient civil-service administration.

Frederick Harbison and Charles Myers, in their study, *Education, Manpower and Economic Growth*, developed a 'Composite Index' to distinguish countries in terms of four levels of human-resources development: Level (I) underdeveloped; (II) partially developed; (III) semi-advanced; and Level (IV) advanced. In describing Level (I) countries they stated that 'at least a third of the stock of high level manpower is employed in the government services and education.' They also indicated that a country is underdeveloped when more than half of its high-level manpower is non-indigenous.[1] It is worth mentioning here that the number of Kuwaitis in the labor force in the high-level manpower bracket is only 3,488 compared with 20,962 non-Kuwaitis, 16.6 per cent of the labor force.

It should be pointed out here that the *effectiveness* of the high-level manpower doesn't depend solely on its increasing numbers but rather on the social system in which it operates. Thus high-level manpower in the bureaucracy can be effective and more productive or less productive depending on the social environment in the country.

It would be important to conduct a survey on the civil-service bureaucracy to find out the relationship, if any, between productivity and education. Such an evaluation study could be carried out by the proposed manpower center.

A field study of occupation adjustment in Kuwait, showed that the educated people in Kuwait adjust better than the less educated ones, and also reported that those in administrative and supervisory positions in the government adjusted to and liked their job more than the clerical workers and manual workers.[2] We can deduce from this study that there is widespread dissatisfaction and difficulty in adjustment among the less educated civil employees. It is important to retrain these people either at work or outside work by providing them with educational facilities and an incentive for acquiring further education.

Since 'managerial manpower' is essential for building economic and social organizations for national development,[3] it is advisable for

90

Kuwait to concentrate on managerial manpower as a number-one priority, because a good managerial staff can effectively utilize the labor resources in the country. Kuwait University and universities abroad can prepare students for management tasks, but turning students into managers will only take place at work through on-the-job management training. Thus it is advisable that newly graduated Kuwaitis be distributed in all sectors of the economy, both public and private.

Attention must also be paid to the non-Kuwaiti population. As explained, the non-Kuwaiti administrators in the service sector, although qualified, feel insecure, unstable and alienated because of the government's policy of 'Kuwaitization', which means replacing the expatriate employee, especially at the administrative level, with native Kuwaitis. This policy has long-range implications because not many of the newly graduated Kuwaitis appointed to administrative-level jobs are well qualified: needless to say, merely being Kuwaiti and holding a university degree does not automatically make one a good administrator. Current policy would appear politically motivated to satisfy the discontent amongst young Kuwaiti graduates by appointing them to high positions. Appointing Kuwaitis to high positions is not inherently a bad thing, of course, but such a step should be introduced gradually so that the new graduates learn the skills and tasks necessary for efficient management. Furthermore, such a policy will create a new class of Kuwaitis and a proletariat class of non-Kuwaitis — a situation which might gradually lead to lower productivity and alienation of the majority of the labor force employed in government. It is not possible to improve the productivity of the foreign labor force without first improving its well-being, through providing security, housing and equal pay for equal work.

The policy of pleasing the 'graduate Kuwaitis' by appointing them to high positions has already led to conflict between two generations of Kuwaitis. As the young, newly graduated Kuwaitis come to work in the civil service, they want to replace the old Kuwaitis who are less educated though more experienced. To aid new blood, the government introduced an early-retirement plan for Kuwaitis at age 45. By this the government provided ten years advance payment for every person willing to retire, and a full retirement pension. It is regrettable that a country suffering from a shortage of manpower should waste in this way a considerable number of its experienced citizens. In this regard, a program could and should be developed to retrain retiring employees to fill other positions in the work force where there is a deficiency in indigenous manpower.

*Toward manpower planning in Kuwait*

This policy of early retirement has not solved the problem of Kuwaiti manpower. Within the last few years, as the number of graduates has increased, a new conflict has developed between the earlier graduates and the new graduates, because most of the administrative jobs are already filled. In an attempt to please everybody, the government created new titles such as Undersecretary of the Ministry, more than three or four Assistant Undersecretaries beneath him. There are also Directors, Assistant Directors, Heads of Department and Assistant Heads[4] The over-employment of Kuwaitis in the government sector is the result of a government policy of guaranteed jobs for every Kuwaiti citizen regardless of his or her qualifications. This has created a huge bureaucracy in the government and increased costs and salaries (see table 5.2).

**Table 5.2**  *Salaries and wages in the government sector, 1965-75 (KD)*

| Year | Number employed | Salaries and wages | Index 1965 = 100.0 Employment | Wages | Average (KD) |
|------|------|------|------|------|------|
| 1965 | 66,641 | 73,299,807 | 100.0 | 100.0 | 1099.9 |
| 1966 | 71,814 | 81,478,897 | 107.8 | 111.6 | 1134.6 |
| 1967 | 76,497 | 90,843,314 | 114.8 | 123.9 | 1187.5 |
| 1968 | 79,287 | 95,647,800 | 119.0 | 130.5 | 1206.3 |
| 1969 | 81,233 | 102,168,643 | 121.9 | 139.4 | 1257.7 |
| 1970 | 82,277 | 107,297,814 | 123.5 | 146.4 | 1304.1 |
| 1971 | 91,706 | 148,032,901 | 137.6 | 202.0 | 1614.2 |
| 1972 | 97,931 | 153,233,280 | 147.0 | 209.1 | 1564.7 |
| 1973 | 104,797 | 163,065,110 | 157.3 | 222.5 | 1556.1 |
| 1974 | 111,573 | 168,617,000 | 167.4 | 241.9 | 1511.3 |
| 1975 | 124,781 | 225,896,971 | 187.2 | 308.2 | 1810.3 |

Source: Ministry of Planning, Central Statistical Office, *Annual Statistical Abstract 1976*, table 65.

Table 5.2 shows that the number of employees almost doubled during the period 1965-75 whilst wages increased more than three times. What is interesting is that the increase in employment was gradual until 1973, when employment jumped by 8,000 people: and by 1975 the number of new employees had jumped by 13,208. The reasons for this sudden increase was the rise in oil prices after 1973-4. Such a trend in government employment forces the government to spend more and more on wages and salaries. This in turn forces the government to produce more oil, which is a violation of its policy of conservation.

To reduce over-employment in the government sector and to up-grade the quality of civil employees, it is essential to introduce in-service training programs. Such programs are important in reducing the high illiteracy rate in the sector. Promotional rewards need to be given as an incentive to those civil employees who are willing to improve their educational and technical level.

It is ironic that the best-qualified Kuwaiti technicians, who have the knowledge and the qualifications to teach others, end up taking jobs as administrators instead of technical trainees or on-the-job training supervisors.

Another method for better educating the civil employee would be for Kuwait University to open itself to civil employees to attend as part-time students. At present, many civil employees are enrolled in part-time education at the Arab University of Beirut.

The shortage of Kuwaiti manpower in other sectors of the economy should make it easy for the government to disperse its employees to other sectors after retraining them and finding jobs for them in the private sector. The widespread invisible under-employment in the civil service should make the government more willing to employ the surplus manpower in these other sectors, and it should start with joint-sector companies because it owns half of the stock. The private sector must take an active role in training and employing Kuwaitis but this cannot be done without an overall economic plan.

At present, policy makers in Kuwait continue to be vague on the drafting of an economic plan. Two separate schools of thought prevail in Kuwait. The influential Financial Elite argues that Kuwait can prosper and develop only through the building of an adequate portfolio of investment as a partial substitute to depletable natural resources.[5] The other dominant group maintains that Kuwait cannot develop economically unless it owns all of its natural resources, and it calls for nationalization of the oil industry and for limitation of foreign companies' operations within Kuwait. This group is represented by leftist members in the National Assembly.[6] (Although the National Assembly has been closed since 1976, as of February 1980 the government has appointed a constitutional committee as a prelude to the re-opening of the National Assembly. It is expected that national elections will take place in the fall of 1980).

The first group envisions Kuwait as a growing financial center. Its argument against industry is that it does not and will not have a comparative advantage.[7] This is based upon assumptions relating to exchange rates, inflation and/or deflation. It is a well known fact that the

93

oil-producing states have been losing money because of their investments abroad:[8]

> Over the past year, our sheikh's sterling investment will have steadily lost out to a comparable dollars investment. By June last year, the relative loss would have been $680,000, by December it would have increased to $2.4 million and by now our sheikh would be starting $3.2 million worse off.

Turning to the second group it was the National Assembly that rejected in principle participation with the oil companies and instead asked for complete takeover (nationalization).[9]

This counter elite is composed mainly of middle and upper middle-class Kuwaitis, most of whom are young and well educated. In ideology they support the Arab Nationalist Movement and they were part of the opposition group in the National Assembly in Kuwait prior to its dissolution in 1976. The counter elite perceives Kuwait developing through furthering closer ties with other Arab states and with Third World countries. It wants Kuwait to industrialize and to build a strong working class through the development of human resources, for Kuwaitis and non-Kuwaitis alike. This group enjoys great support from labor unions and student organizations.

The weakness of the 'counter elite' lies in its lack of a genuine study of 'economic feasibility' for industrializing Kuwait. It tends to over-emphasize 'industrialization' without taking into consideration the social implications, and how one is to change the prevailing attitudes in Kuwait. This problem was underlined in an SRI report, where it was argued that 'If Kuwait intends to develop modern industry that competes internationally, some of those attitudes and behavioral patterns that contribute to producing an industrial society must be developed.'[10]

The Kuwaiti government has taken a middle-of-the-road approach between the two groups. While it continues to invest money abroad it has also begun a process of limited industrialization. The creation of the Industrial Bank in 1974 was one step in that direction. At the inauguration of the bank, the prime minister stated:[11]

> In its effort to bolster the industrial sector of our country, the Government has aimed at the building of a national economy based on firm foundations by diversifying national sources of income and the construction of industries in order to absorb the Kuwaiti labor force, and finding alternate outlets for investment.

## Reforming the educational system

The need of the less developed countries for skilled and professional manpower requires a substantial change in their educational and training programs. People must be trained to meet the necessary social and labor-market requirements.[12] Social, political and economic development cannot be achieved without first changing the attitudes of the population concerned.

The contribution that education can make to the development of Kuwait cannot be over-emphasized. Kuwait is faced with critical decisions on its choice of education, dependent on the types of changes the country wishes to effect.

The types of education a student should be exposed to is one of the most important questions confronting the developing countries. The educational system should adapt to the changing needs of society: in other words, it should always be flexible enough to adapt to changing circumstances. Improvements in education need not mean expanding schools and increasing enrollment, but rather changing the content of the educational system. Myrdal was correct when he argued that the allocation of resources to education cannot be divorced from the content of education:[13]

> In general, educational policy must have the central purpose of directing and apportioning educational efforts so as to give a maximum impetus to national development. The problem of reforming education in South Asia is far from being merely a quantitative one of providing more schools; it is as much or more a problem of eliminating miseducation and large scale waste of educational resources. What is needed is not simply an expansion of educational facilities and their reapportioning to serve the various age groups, both sexes, and all social classes, but a more purposive selection of knowledge and skills thought [sic], the attitudes implanted and the learning methods employed.

As in the rest of the less developed countries and some other Arab countries, the curriculum in Kuwait tends to be highly theoretical and largely irrelevant, and the graduates tend to be of low quality.[14] It is doubtful, indeed, whether the educational system of Kuwait is adequate for a nation confronted with a manpower shortage. For example, in the three levels of Kuwait's educational system (primary, intermediate, and secondary), 70 per cent of the curriculum is devoted to the study of humanities, while only 30 per cent is devoted to the sciences.[15]

Until 1976 the curriculum at Kuwait University only offered courses in liberal arts and education. Here again Kuwait is similar in its educational gap to other less developed countries. As explained by Lipset:[16]

> Another major problem of Latin American universities is the curricula and status orientation of students which encourage vast numbers to work for degrees in subjects which are not needed in large quantity. Educational policy often encourages such maladjustment by making it much easier to secure a degree in subjects such as Law or the Humanities, rather than the sciences or engineering.

Thus a revision of curricula and teaching methods must be made to incorporate recent technological advances and Kuwait's need for scientifically orientated manpower. This is a necessity that cannot be stressed enough. The educational system must be orientated toward the country's manpower needs.

At the present time the major policy emphasis is academic, so that what is needed now is a reorientation in the educational system. High-school education should be designed to prepare students not only for university-level work but also for entry into technical and teaching colleges. An optional range of courses in the fields of science and teaching must be provided within a single school, rather than to proliferate specialized institutions.[17] The advantage of such a program is that it reduces the cost of establishing new, specialized institutions and, more importantly, in the long run it changes people's attitudes toward technical training. The graduates of such schools have the option of continuing their academic program or joining other, higher technical schools abroad.

Improving the quality of education in Kuwait is not an easy task because most of the teachers are Arabs who have come from less developed countries. Although well qualified, they teach in a very regimented way.[18] 'Another feature of the Egyptian educational system has been its high degree of centralized and routinized administration. . . . The curriculum of the schools was characterized by a regimentation which was almost military in character.' Another author described the educational system in the Arab countries in the following way: 'The French models of Education which are being abolished in France still remain in the Arab world.'[19] One can see that human development in Kuwait will not be an easy or simple task because to educate people one must have adequately trained teachers; and to have adequately trained teachers there must be high-quality teacher education. Therefore it will be necessary to improve the caliber of teaching staff at

Kuwait University and to retrain the present teachers in the public schools. Such a task should not be too difficult because Kuwait has experience with such retraining programs. During the early 1970s, for example, the Ministry of Education decided to adopt the 'new maths' for the public schools in Kuwait and a program of retraining for the Kuwaiti and non-Kuwaiti teacher was carried out with great success.

While the educational system is seen by many Kuwaitis as one of the avenues of social and economic mobility, the motivation to finish school is higher among well-to-do families. In a study conducted by the Stanford Research Institute it was found that: 'in spite of equal educational opportunities, children from the richest quartile of both Kuwaiti and non-Kuwaiti families receive almost twice the educational benefits as children from the poorest quartile.'[20] To change such a situation, the government must carry out a special educational program to help those underprivileged people who drop out of school, by either providing them with on-the-job educational training or putting restrictions and educational qualifications on government employment.

The high drop-out rate is very much related to widespread illiteracy. It is advisable to use the mass media, especially television and radio, to help in this regard. A literacy campaign for adult education should be the state's first priority because children of illiterate parents will undoubtedly fall behind and drop out of school. Furthermore, an extensive adult-education program will have an immediate impact on Kuwait's development.

## Vocational and technical education

The problems of vocational and technical education as a source of skilled manpower extend beyond limited enrollment. Many vocational-training institutes opened hastily and lack adequate curricula in terms of the needs of Kuwait. Students graduating from such institutions are not necessarily equipped to perform necessary functions in society. As explained in chapter 4, Kuwait has had bad experiences with vocational training. The graduates from such institutions are, in many cases, not qualified to handle the job they have supposedly been trained to perform, and the government is forced to send many of them abroad for further training. The government is thus aware of the problem.

An example of the problems was provided when graduates of the Business Institute attempted to enroll in Kuwait University for the academic year 1977–8. The university refused to accept them, arguing that they should go into the job market where there was a need for them. Furthermore, it was argued, if the university accepted these students then what had been the purpose of the Business Institute?[21]

Since the vocational and technical-education program in Kuwait is not adequate, there is an urgent need to improve the system, and Kuwait should consult indigenous as well as outside experts for advice in this area. Here again special attention should be paid to improving the quality of the teaching.

The problem of people's reluctance to undertake vocational training should be one of the country's first priorities. To overcome the lack of interest in technical and vocational training there is a need to change people's attitudes and habits. Such a task will not be easy but educating children at an early age to the needs of such skills is important. The mass media should be utilized to correct the widely held belief that technical education is socially unacceptable and economically unrewarding. The government must take the lead in giving financial reward to graduates of technical college by making it equivalent to a university degree.

The private sector in Kuwait must take an interest in vocational education by opening schools and training institutes of better quality. Such a step would have two purposes: first, the private sector knows exactly what its own needs are and could therefore adjust such institutions accordingly; secondly, such a step would ensure the quality of the graduates, since the private sector would be investing money in such a program and would want, therefore, to be sure that trainees were adequate.

The government must utilize the multinational corporations. There should be a program providing government contracts to these companies for the training of Kuwaiti nationals. Furthermore, these corporation programs should cost less and be of a higher quality due to the experience of the multinationals. Another important aspect of such a program would be that the prospective trainees would be exposed to new and more appropriate sets of values in modern institutions as a result of their contact with foreign training.

Since the cost of vocational and technical education in Kuwait is very high, and the quality low, it is advisable to send Kuwaiti students abroad for vocational training. At present the quality of education in the developed countries is much better than that provided locally. Technical students should be sent for study abroad at an early date and not after they graduate from Kuwaiti schools. In addition to utilizing foreign institutions, there should be a concerted effort to improve local institutions. The success of technical education will depend greatly on the dual approach of fulfilling immediate needs by sending students abroad and by improving local institutions. In addition the government must make a concerted national effort to achieve a more efficient balance between academic and technical education.

## Women's participation in the labor force

Before we discuss the possibility of increasing women's participation in the labor force, it is useful to review the status of women prior to the discovery of oil and the role they played in society. We also need to understand the social and cultural forces that prevent women from fully participating in the labor force. After this analysis we can come to a more realistic appraisal of the problems underlying the low participation of women in the labor force.

Prior to the discovery of oil in Kuwait in the late 1930s, women were not active in the traditional society of Kuwait. Their role was confined to raising children and taking care of the house. This passive role was maintained even when the men were absent for five months each year when they went pearl-diving, from May to September. Superstition and belief in magic were widespread among Kuwaiti women, who were both illiterate and ignorant.[22] The discovery of oil and the consequent expansion of the economy, with universal education for both males and females, have contributed greatly to the increasing number of females in the labor force over the last twenty years. The number of Kuwaiti women in the labor force is nevertheless very low (see table 5.3).

Table 5.3 indicates that the number of females in the labor force increased slowly and is still very low. It is important to note that while the number of non-Kuwaiti females is smaller, their participation rate is much higher, because economic necessity has forced them to seek work. Thus the non-Kuwaiti female has the incentive and motivation for work which her Kuwaiti counterpart lacks.

Another interesting aspect of table 5.3 is the fact that although Kuwaiti women's participation rate increased slowly during the period 1957–70, their number increased more than threefold in the five years 1970–5 and their participation rate more than doubled. The reasons for such a sudden jump in the 1970s can be traced to several factors:

**Table 5.3** *Women in the labor force, by nationality and participation rate*

|  | *Kuwaiti* | *non-Kuwaiti* | *Total* |
|---|---|---|---|
| *1957* |  |  |  |
| Population | 53,135 | 16,868 | 70,003 |
| Labor force | 384 | 1,693 | 2,077 |
| Participation rate | 0.7 | 1.0 | 3.0 |
| *1965* |  |  |  |
| Population | 107,490 | 73,537 | 181,027 |
| Labor force | 1,092 | 7,676 | 8,768 |
| Participation rate | 1.0 | 10.4 | 4.8 |
| *1970* |  |  |  |
| Population | 171,883 | 146,898 | 318,781 |
| Labor force | 2,055 | 14,542 | 16,597 |
| Participation rate | 1.2 | 9.9 | 5.2 |
| *1975* |  |  |  |
| Population | 235,488 | 215,581 | 451,069 |
| Labor force | 7,477 | 27,729 | 35,206 |
| Participation rate | 3.2 | 12.9 | 7.8 |

Source: Ministry of Planning, *Annual Statistical Abstract 1976*, table 54.

(1)　There were more females attending school;

(2)　the social barriers against working women became less restricted;

(3)　high inflation in Kuwait forced many middle-class females to enter the labor force to supplement their husband's income.

Women's participation in the labor force is not only low but their occupational choice is limited, by custom and tradition, to the fields of education, health and social welfare. For example, in 1973 out of 5,200 working women there were 5,000 working for the government and only 200 in the private sector. A field study on Kuwaiti attitudes toward working women in Kuwait indicated that the majority of people in the sample (69 per cent) agreed that women should work, while 30 per cent were against the idea. However, when those who agreed were asked to specify the jobs they preferred women to work at, 90 per cent said they preferred the government, and more specifically education, because in the Ministry of Education there is no integration between male and female (see table 5.4).

What is interesting about table 5.4 is the fact that the majority of males (53.1 per cent) disapproves of integration between male and female. They prefer women to work in the government as teachers. Thus, while Kuwaiti males want women to work, they still want them

100

**Table 5.4**  *Preference for government jobs*

| Reason | Male No. | % | Female No. | % | Total No. | % |
|---|---|---|---|---|---|---|
| More security | 38 | 26.6 | 50 | 40.3 | 88 | 33.0 |
| Less hours | 17 | 11.9 | 10 | 8.06 | 27 | 10.1 |
| No integration between sexes | 76 | 53.1 | 49 | 39.5 | 125 | 46.8 |
| Other reasons | 12 | 8.4 | 15 | 12.09 | 27 | 10.1 |
| Total | 143 | | 124 | | 267 | |

Source: Fahad Al Thakeb, 'Mawqef al Kuwaityeen Min MaKanet al Marah fee al Kuwaiti' (Kuwaiti Stand on the Position of Women), paper presented to the Arab Women Regional Conference, April 1975.

confined to the fields of education and health. It is a deeply rooted attitude among many males in Kuwaiti society that if women work they should perform certain types of jobs. There is a need to change this attitude toward women by educating children that women are not that different from men.

The question arises here of why educated females continue to accept this pattern of employment. Aside from societal restrictions, there is no doubt that educational institutions, where the girls receive a great deal of their socialization, are not reformist.

It is important here to ask the question of what prevents women in Kuwait from taking an active role in the labor force. There are social, economic and political reasons for their low participation in the labor force — the most obvious reason being the widespread traditional thinking that views a woman's place as at home raising children. The source of traditional thought is very much influenced by Islam. H.A.R. Gibb sees Islam itself as a revealed religion which sought to impose on a tribal society a 'family concept' in which women were given the same rights, although admittedly not to the same degree, as men. The intent was to encourage a true partnership between the sexes and make property familial rather than to have it belong to the tribal unit. Before Islam, despite certain exceptional cases, women had no rights and no independent status, but with Islam the dowry remained hers, and she could inherit. What made Islam more conservative with regard to women than had originally been intended was the pressure of the ideal of tribal honor stimulated by early and widespread conquest of early Islam. It is to this that Gibb attributes the fact that divorce, condemned by the Prophet, became a common practice in Islam, and that women were submitted to the veil and to the harem, and that polygamy, originally permitted, though reluctantly and with a maximum of four wives, became an accepted institution.[23] Islamic law gives the father, brother, uncle and grandfather (the guardian) the right to accept or reject the female's marriage without her permission. This is very well stated in Article 12 of Personal Statute Law in Kuwait:[24]

> Marriage of the virgin, the minor, previously married women, and those in a similar status shall not be performed except with the permission of her father or grandfather who is not opposed to her marriage.

The women's organization in Kuwait[25] is trying to change this law by giving women the right to decide for themselves. As they state:[26]

> A – The Guardian shall have the right to initiate the marriage of his protege if she did not complete twenty-one calendar years of age, after obtaining her approval and consent. If he blocks her she may raise her case to the judge to authorize her marriage, but if she is already over twenty-one years of age she then may authorize her marriage by herself.
> B – In order to legalize or sanction the marriage contract it shall be required that the wife's age be not below sixteen calendar years and the husband's age not below eighteen calendar years at the same time of legalization.

It is not likely that the government will accept such a moderate modification, because Islamic Law is not to be challenged. A woman in Kuwait cannot legally obtain the right to divorce her husband. The social status of women remains low in Kuwait and they are still subservient to males.

The problem in Kuwait is not only that society is traditional but also that the policy makers enhance this tradition by a policy of segregation between males and females. For example, in Kuwait University males and females attend classes separately, although the campus is integrated. When separation became formally institutionalized, its effects were very harmful. Segregated courses are still prevalent in Kuwait University despite some professors' attempts to integrate male and female students in one classroom. It is worth mentioning here that segregation in Kuwait University not only costs the state a great amount of money (such as building two university campuses instead of one) but also increases the demand for more qualified manpower as teachers. This policy also puts great pressure on the existing teachers and forces them to give the same lecture twice. This takes valuable time from their research.

102

## Economic factors

The economic factors that prevent full female participation in the labor force are very much related to the social aspects. The relationship between the particular structure of control and women's participation in the labor force is considerable. In the Middle East, control over women is monopolized by the kinship network, and female seclusion is legitimized in terms of family honor and esteem. Thus economic propositions are made for relatives at all times regardless of their marital status. As stated by Nadia Yousseff:[27]

> In the Middle East, which depends entirely upon kinship and the
> family as a basis of social organization, kinship institutions provide
> that there is always a male member (father, brother, cousin or
> uncle) who is economically, legally, and morally responsible for the
> woman, whatever her marital status. This is true of all social classes.

Undoubtedly the policy of 'social welfare' and the guarantee of a job for every Kuwaiti perpetuates male domination because many Kuwaiti males feel that since they have a steady income (government job) there is no need for their wife or sister to work. In a traditional society like Kuwait the men are expected to support their wives, mothers and sisters, thus reducing the incentive for women to seek work. It is fair to state that, as long as women remain dependent on men, the likelihood of large numbers of females entering the labor market will remain small.

## Political factors

Any serious attempt to increase women's participation in the labor force must consider in addition the position of women in general and their political rights in particular. Any increase in women's participation in the labor force will depend greatly on the decision-makers in the country and how they perceive the role of women. At present decision-makers continue to perceive the major role of women as taking care of home and family. Thus there is an inherent contradiction between their set goals of increasing women's participation and their insistence that a woman's first duty is 'at home as wife and mother.'[28]

Women in Kuwait have no political rights. They cannot nominate themselves or elect anyone to public office as stated in the National Assembly Election Law of 1962. Article 1 states:

> Every Kuwaiti male over 21 years has the right to elect: excluded from this category: the naturalized citizen who has been in the country less than 20 years.

It is rather clear here that political rights are limited to Kuwaiti male citizens. Not only are Kuwaiti women excluded but also newly naturalized citizens. One wonders why women are excluded and what is the basis for such law. David Gordon argues that the basis for the rejection of women's rights to vote or to serve as deputies in Parliament is the statement in the Koran (XXXIII:133) 'Remain in your homes: Do not exhibit yourselves as did the women in the times of Ignorance.' The 'Ulema' (religious authorities) state: 'This citation proves that it is the duty of a woman to do everything to safeguard her honor and reputation. It proves that women must be kept from temptation and prevented from being a temptation to others.'[29]

In *Beyond the Veil*, Fatima Mernissi states that:[30]

> Contrary to what is commonly assumed, Islam does not advance the thesis of women's inherent inferiority. Quite the contrary, it affirms the potential equality between the sexes. The existing inequality does not rest on an ideological or biological theory of women's inferiority, but is the outcome of specific social institutions designed to restrain her power, namely segregation and legal subordination of the women to the men in the family structure.

One wonders if women were given the right to vote in Kuwait, whether that would lead to an increase in their participation in the labor force? One cannot expect to effect such an increase without first giving women full equality with men, by integrating them fully in social, economic and political life. Providing women with political rights is but a first step toward their economic independence and liberty.

What policies should be adopted to increase women's participation in the labor force? First there must be a change in society's perceptions and attitudes toward working women. This can be done through changes in the educational system, which portrays women as weak and dependent on men. A large number of Kuwaiti females have been socialized to consider work outside their home undesirable. It is necessary to conduct study and research to determine how to modify such attitudes.

The illiteracy rate among Kuwaiti females is still very high, despite the fact that more and more enroll in schools every year (see chapter 4). According to the 1975 census, the illiteracy rate among Kuwaiti females was 59.1 per cent, a high percentage for a small country like Kuwait.

Therefore the state's first priority in this respect should be to eliminate illiteracy among females. An illiteracy campaign should be carried out using radio and television.

The importance of women's education goes further than increasing their number in the labor force. An educated mother will help and push her children to attend school. It is recommended that special adult-education programs with their own well qualified staff should undertake the task of raising the educational level of mothers. The content of the curriculum and approach to the material in adult education should be different from that for children. Currently this is not the case.

In the field of general education, Kuwait has made great strides. What remains to be seen is whether or not education will help to improve the status of women in general and encourage them to participate in the labor force.

In the field of vocational and technical education, female opportunities are limited to four out of the ten institutions: nursing, telecommunications, health, and vocational and technical education for females. Access to these institutions is quite an improvement on the past. Janice Terry, commenting on the newly rich traditional states, notes:[31]

> It is ironic that these traditionally conservative areas will probably surpass those Arab nations with longer histories of educating women (i.e., Jordan and Egypt), but which lack the monetary wherewithal to support further educational programmes or to finance education at the same level as their wealthier brothers.

It is worth mentioning here that the number of female students attending technical and vocational education in 1975–6 was 1,308, while the number in intermediate and secondary school was 41,061. One of the reasons for the reluctance to enter technical and vocational school is basically the same as that of men: it is viewed as socially undesirable. A second reason lies in the students' awareness of the low quality of these schools. UNESCO criticized the technical high schools in Kuwait and recommended that they should be integrated with general education.[32]

Finally, if the government seriously wants more female participation in the labor force, then it must work toward achieving such goals by providing the following:

(1)  Elimination of the rules and regulations which prevent women from participating fully in society, and the granting to women of the same rights as men, i.e., full political rights, the freedom to choose their own spouse without the parental intervention, and the right to divorce.

(2)  Provision of help for those who drop out of school, by giving them alternative educational opportunities.

(3)  Responsible, high-level government positions for women. There are many Kuwaiti women who are more qualified than men in terms of educational status and seniority in the government but who rarely hold a high post in the government. If women are allowed to hold high posts in the government, the public image of women will gradually change, and it will further give women self-confidence.

(4)  Incentives for the working women of Kuwait by the opening of a day-care center for women with children.

(5)  A 'women research center' to be attached to the manpower center.

## Reforming the Nationality Law

Throughout this study an attempt has been made to explain the causes of the manpower problem in Kuwait, and the increasing dependence on an expatriate labor force which in most cases resides in Kuwait only for prescribed periods of time (i.e., until the work ends) and then returns home.

Undoubtedly the high turnover rate of skilled and unskilled manpower impedes economic and social development in the country. This problem will grow, for government studies indicate that Kuwait's dependence on foreign labor will increase rather than decrease. The Ministry of Planning indicates that Kuwaitis will comprise 29.1 per cent of the labor force in 1981, while non-Kuwaitis will comprise 70.9 per cent (table 5.5). Thus the number of non-Kuwaitis in the labor force will be more than twice that of Kuwaitis. The manpower problems will exacerbate other problems if Kuwait continues its policy of discrimination and alienation of the majority of its population and labor force (i.e., expatriate labor), and the Kuwaiti nationals continue to receive special status in every aspect of life. It will increase tension and resentment between the two communities in the country and it may well be the source of social and political instability. To avoid such problems there is a need to review and reform the existing nationality laws.

In 1959, in order to ensure proper rights for Kuwaiti citizens, the government issued the Nationality Law, which states in Article 1:[33]

> The Kuwaitis are basically those people who inhabited Kuwait before 1920 and have continued to reside there until the date of publication of this law.

**Table 5.5**  *Population and labor force, 1980–1 (in thousands)*

|  | Kuwaiti | | | non-Kuwaiti | | | Total | | |
|---|---|---|---|---|---|---|---|---|---|
|  | *Male* | *Female* | *Total* | *Male* | *Female* | *Total* | *Male* | *Female* | *Total* |
| Population | 325.1 | 323.7 | 648.8 | 408.0 | 365.4 | 773.4 | 733.1 | 689.1 | 1,422.2 |
| Labor force | 109.5 | 10.1 | 119.6 | 244.7 | 47.9 | 292.6 | 354.2 | 58.0 | 412.2 |

Source: Ministry of Planning, *Five Year Plan 1977–81*, Government Printing, 1977.

Native Kuwaitis are those people who have lived in Kuwait since or from before 1920, and their offspring. They are the people who enjoy full political rights, such as the privilege to vote for the National Assembly and municipality, and to be eligible for nomination and election to public office.

It is worth mentioning here that in order for a foreigner to qualify for Kuwaiti nationality, he must have resided in Kuwait continuously for at least fifteen years. The Nationality Law was revised in 1966 to state that Kuwaiti nationality can be granted to those Arabs who have resided in Kuwait since 1945, and to non-Arabs who have resided in Kuwait since 1930. Citizens by 'naturalization' are discriminated against by law: for example, they are allowed to vote but they cannot run for public office.

Article 4 of the Law also gives the Minister of the Interior the power to give Kuwaiti nationality to every Arab and non-Arab who has resided in Kuwait continuously for ten years and fifteen years respectively, starting from the publication of the Law in 1959.

Kuwaiti nationality is not granted automatically to those who fulfill the requirements of residency. They must also fulfill certain additional requirements and procedures such as entering the country legally and being of good character.

Article 4 of the Nationality Law is one of the causes of the manpower problem in Kuwait because it specifies that only fifty people can be naturalized each year. Article 5, Law Number 6 of 1966, however, gives the government the power to grant Kuwaiti nationality to everyone who served the country and who deserves nationality.[34] The government has used and continues to use this clause in the law to grant nationality to thousands of Bedouin Arabs who have come to Kuwait from Saudi Arabia and other parts of the Arabian desert.

The question might be posed here as to why the Kuwaiti government, suffering from a shortage of skilled manpower, has granted citizenship to such a large number of illiterate and unskilled Arab nomads, while on the other hand restricting naturalization of skilled and professional Arabs? One answer to this question is political: the Arab nomads (Bedouins) are extremely loyal to the royal family because of the tribal linkage to it. This policy, moreover, has been perpetuated by the government in order to counteract the growing discontent among the urban population who, for the most part, are better educated and hold a more liberal outlook. This government policy is rather shortsighted and may backfire. Presently, this population of Bedouins is easily satisfied through employment in the Army and police force, and with being granted low-income housing. This situation is bound to alter as soon as the parents and their children become urbanized and more educated.

The other reason for the naturalization of Bedouins is the fear that the foreign urban population might introduce new ideas or thoughts that would disrupt the existing traditional pattern, as explained by Frank Stoakes:[35]

> Oil revenues and the development projects they finance, combined with the initial barrenness of indigenous culture, may lead – as most notoriously in Kuwait – to a vast influx of foreigners. Some of these represent that regional body of floating labor which is a feature of the Gulf littoral, or are drawn from the Persian Proletariat: these may introduce ideas of labor organization and action, and in some cases affiliations with politically oriented labour movements in the Arab world or with movements allied to Communism. Others are from more advanced Arab countries, and these present major problems if they are granted naturalization in great numbers. They threaten to change indigenous culture in a way that is initially unacceptable to rulers and public alike. If they are denied it, they may become an element of political opposition and a channel of domestic or foreign subversion.

Much traditional concern has been expressed over the possibility of Kuwaitis experiencing a quantitative or qualitative decrease in benefits if forced to share them with a great number of expatriates. Given Kuwait's oil revenues, this would seem unlikely. Thus, it appears that Kuwait has two choices with regard to naturalization and accommodation of the expatriate labor force:

(1)  To continue its present policy of exclusion of the majority of the population, i.e., non-Bedouin foreigners. In this case, social and political unrest might flare up because of the policy of non-integration of a large segment of society and discrimination against these individuals regarding salaries and other social benefits (see chapter 3).

(2)  To reform the Nationality Law to accommodate some of those people the country needs for their professional services.

Since it is difficult to grant citizenship to every expatriate in the labor force, I suggest the following method for granting nationality:

(1)  Since Kuwait's population is small and in need of a large number of skilled individuals, Kuwaiti nationality should be granted to all educated Arabs who have emigrated outside the Arab world to such countries as the USA and Canada and the western European

countries. These educated and skilled Arabs could be of great benefit to Kuwait in its difficult task of development.

(2) Concerning the expatriate labor presently in Kuwait a more flexible policy of residency should be adopted. Kuwait should grant permanent residency to the qualified manpower and it should grant them nationality after ten years of continued residency. The government should also provide them with social security and retirement benefits after they become permanent residents. A person should reside in Kuwait for at least five years before becoming eligible for permanent residency.

(3) Since the majority of the expatriate labor in Kuwait is Palestinian Arabs who have no homeland, Kuwait should utilize such skilled and well qualified people by providing them with permanent residency, if they wish, since such a step may clash with national objectives of the Palestinians to return to their homeland. This should be provided for all Palestinians presently in Kuwait, and Kuwaiti nationality should also be given to those whose skills and services are badly needed in Kuwait. Such a policy would add to the security and comfort of these people, who would thereby be more productive.

Many Palestinian Arabs were born and raised in Kuwait, and their parents participated in the development of the country. Thus it is logical that they should be given permanent residency and granted the right to own property. It is a well-known fact in Kuwait that Palestinian children are considered to be the best students; and in a *New York Times* article it was reported that 48 of the top 50 high-school science students were Palestinian.[36] Therefore the state should utilize such available manpower by taking the responsibility in granting them scholarships for further education abroad, so that when they come back they provide their services to Kuwait. These benefits should also be extended to the already available supply of qualified manpower – the expatriates, especially the Palestinian Arab students who graduate from Kuwaiti high schools – in order to educate them further and thus better serve Kuwait.

At the present time, these high-school graduates go for further study on their own and end up working in countries other than Kuwait. If Kuwait took the initiative and provided university education for these expatriates' children, they would return to serve in Kuwait. In this way Kuwait could utilize the manpower that it already has. At present, entry into Kuwait University follows strict quotas: 50 per cent of the places go to Kuwaiti nationals, 20 per cent to Arabs from the Arabian Gulf states, and the remaining 30 per cent to other Arabs. It is reported that only about 10 per cent of the Palestinians who want to go to college can get into the university.[37] Thus there is a need to reform university-entrance requirements, which should be based on a student's qualifications and not a student's nationality.

(4)  The issue of residency and nationality should be handled by a committee of experts (preferably from the Manpower Center) to study Kuwait's manpower needs and recommend its findings to the government.

## Manpower Center

Manpower policy and function is presently decentralized and scattered among various ministries and institutions such as:

(1)  The Ministry of Planning, which conducts a population census every five years. Within this ministry there is a manpower department which was created in 1972. This department carries out studies related to manpower, in co-operation with the Central Statistical Office.

(2)  The Ministry of Social Affairs and Labor, which is responsible for the registration and issuing of work permits. This ministry also has a manpower division, which carries out other manpower-related research and studies. This ministry is also responsible for some vocational education schools.

(3)  The Ministry of Education, which is responsible for education and vocational training.

(4)  The Ministry of the Interior, which is responsible for issuing entry visas for foreign workers and is also responsible for naturalization and nationality.

(5)  The Central Vocational Training Directorate, which is responsible for co-ordinating the activities of the various vocational programs in Kuwait.

(6)  The Kuwait Arab Planning Institute, which conducts various studies related to manpower and the training of high-level manpower.

(7)  The Civil Service Department, which is responsible for employment in the government sector.

One of the first tasks in developing a manpower plan is to end the multiplicity of ministries and institutions with responsibility for various aspects of manpower. A 'manpower center' to co-ordinate the various studies, research and other activities related to manpower should be established. The center's objectives would be as follows:

111

(1)   The center would collect information and data related to manpower, then analyse these data before recommending and formulating the necessary course of action to be taken. The center would estimate the future demand of manpower, by sex, occupation, educational level and sector of the economy. Such information is essential in directing the student toward the fields of specialization Kuwait needs in the future.

For proper utilization of manpower, the center would need access to the policy-makers in Kuwait to ensure that its program would be carried out. Furthermore, a good working relationship between the center, the government, and the private sector, also involved in manpower development, would make the center's task easier. A close link between the manpower center and the civil service would need to be established to ensure that the right people were employed in the right place.

(2)   The manpower center would co-ordinate, supervise and upgrade the existing manpower training centers, such as the vocational training programs. In this way the center would carry out or translate its decisions into effective plans of action.

(3)   The center would prepare and direct the new generation for the jobs needed by the economy. This could be done by better co-ordination between educational output and manpower requirement: if the country needed more physical scientists and less social scientists, for example, the educational system would be adjusted accordingly.

(4)   The center would carry out the task of analysing the social and cultural factors that prevent the population from taking certain kinds of jobs (i.e., technical and manual work) whilst preferring government jobs. After isolating the rationale for such an attitude, the center would correct it through education and through the mass media.

(5)   The center would provide advice on educational and training programs. If certain educational programs were inadequate, the center would provide manpower experts to study the reasons.

(6)   The manpower center could provide information on the availability or need for certain kinds of skills for the private sector (Employer Association) and for the trade unions. In turn, the center could also collect information from the business community about their need for certain qualified manpower, so that the center could work to provide such manpower.

(7)   The manpower center could recommend policies to reduce the problem of under-utilization and over-employment that prevails in the government sector, by shifting manpower from one sector to another where there is a shortage (i.e., private sector).

(8)  The center could recommend certain policies and guidelines related to the policy of naturalization according to the country's needs for manpower in specific fields.

(9)  Within the manpower center would be established a 'women's department'. This department would concentrate on increasing women's participation in the labor forces. It could also carry out research and studies related to women. This department could co-ordinate all work related to women in Kuwait. The department would be run by Kuwaiti women who knew first hand the specific problems confronting women in Kuwait today.

(10)  The manpower center would establish close relations with international agencies dealing with manpower, labor and employment, such as the International Labor Organization, the International Bank for Reconstruction and Development, the Agency for International Development, and others. The research of other countries in the fields of human resources development would aid Kuwait.

## Organization of the Center

In terms of organization the center would be linked to the prime minister's office and consist of a board of directors who would outline and co-ordinate the manpower policy. The board of directors would include the following ministries: (a) Planning (b) Education (c) Social Affairs and Labor (d) Interior, and (e) the Head of the Civil Service Department (see figure 5.1). An advisory committee would be linked to the center to provide expertise and knowledge and to advise on the best method to achieve manpower objectives. The advisory committee would consist of the following:

(1)  Kuwait University – the university could provide the qualified manpower to conduct research and study and thus, a representative from the university would be essential.

(2)  The Arab Planning Institute – another well-qualified institute that has already conducted various studies in the manpower field. A representative from this institution would be a great help to the center.

(3)  The private sector – as the government objective now is to diversify the economy, a representative from the private sector would help greatly.

(4)  Women's Council – since a principal goal is to increase women's participation in the labor force, a woman representative should be a necessary part of the center. The women's council could be elected

113

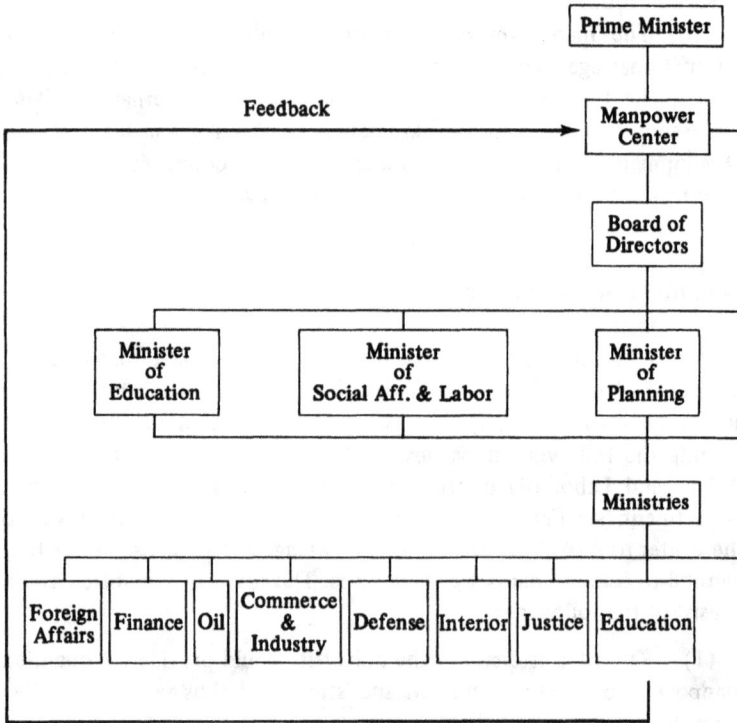

**Figure 5.1** *Organization of Manpower Center*

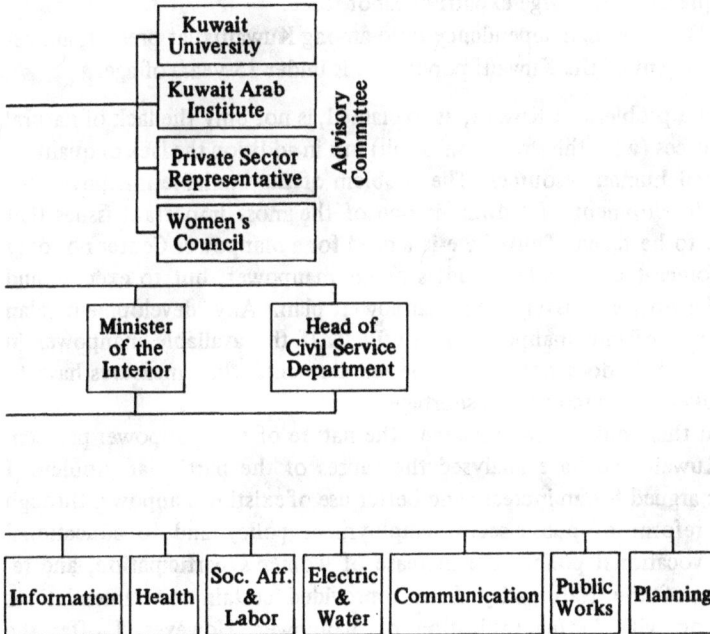

from the Women's Association in Kuwait or selected from other professional women's groups.

## Summary

The policy-makers and planners must bear in mind the specific manpower problem confronting Kuwait:

(1)  The rapid growth of the population in Kuwait, because of the presence of a large expatriate labor force.

(2)  The high dependency ratio among Kuwaitis: at present, almost 50 per cent of the Kuwaiti population is under 15 years of age.

The problem in Kuwait, as explained, is not only the lack of natural resources (with the exception of oil) but in addition the lack of qualified trained human resources. The problem of the available manpower for the development of Kuwait is one of the most important issues that have to be faced. Thus there is a need for a Manpower Center not only to forecast and publish studies about manpower, but to execute and implement effectively the manpower plan. Any development plan requires certain manpower to fulfill it. If the available manpower in the country does not satisfy the requirements, then measures have to be taken to overcome this shortage.

In this book I have explained the nature of the manpower problem in Kuwait and have analysed the causes of the particular problem. I have argued for an increase and better use of existing manpower through the reform of public-sector employment policy and to educational and vocational policy, the increase of women's participation, and reform of the Nationality Law. I provided certain recommendations dealing with better utilization of manpower. However, I offer the creation of a 'manpower center' which I believe would be worth striving for, because the center could be responsible for all aspects of manpower development.

# Notes

**Notes to Introduction**

1  F. Harbison and C. Myers, *Education, Manpower and Economic Growth*, McGraw-Hill, New York, 1964, p. 13.
2  E. Staley, *The Future of Underdeveloped Countries*, Harper & Row, New York, 1954, p. 203.


**Notes to Chapter 1**

1  H. R. P. Dickson, *Kuwait and her Neighbours*, Allen & Unwin, London, 1956, p. 30.
2  State of Kuwait, *The Oil of Kuwait: Facts and Figures* (in Arabic), Ministry of Finance and Oil, 1970, p. 11.
3  A. M. Abu Hakima, *History of Kuwait* (in Arabic), Kuwait Government Press, p. 102. See also Y. Al Somat, *Al Kalej Al Arabi: Derasat Fe Esol Al Sokan (The Arabian Gulf: A Study of Population Origin)*.
4  Stanford Research Institute and the American University, *Area Handbook for the Peripheral States of the Arabian Peninsula*, Government Printing Office, Washington DC, p. 104.
5  M. Al Rumaihi, *Oil and Social Change in the Arabian Gulf* (in Arabic), Institute for Higher Studies, Arab League Office, Cairo, 1975, p. 36.
6  M. Katakura, *Bedouin Village*, University of Tokyo Press, 1977, p. 48.
7  D. Cook, *Kuwait: Miracle on the Desert*, Grosset & Dunlap, New York, 1970, pp. 127–8.
8  R. Patai, *The Arab Mind*, Scribner, New York, 1976, p. 128.
9  A. Aziz Husayn, *Al Mujtama Al Arabi Fe Al Kuwait (Arab Society in Kuwait)*, Institute for Higher Studies, Arab League Office, Cairo, 1960, p. 57.

10  Dickson, op. cit., p. 257.

11  Ibid.

12  H. A. Al Ebraheem, *Kuwait: A Political Study*, Kuwait University, 1975, p. 134.

13  A. I. Baaklini, The Legislature in Kuwait's Political System, unpublished paper, Graduate School of Public Affairs, State University of New York at Albany, p. 7.

14  Al Ebraheem, op. cit., p. 134.

15  Ibid., p. 100.

16  L. Pelly, 'Remarks on the Tribes, Trade and Resources Around the Shore Line of the Persian Gulf,' *Transactions of the Bombay Geographical Society*, vol. xvii, January 1863–December 1864, p. 73.

17  M. Al Qarbali, *Iqtisadyat Al Kuwait (Kuwait's Economy)*, p. 73.

18  A. Al Rashid, *Tarik al Kuwait (History of Kuwait)*, Dar Al Hayat, Beirut, 1971, p. 68.

19  F. Shebab, 'Kuwait: A Super Affluent Society,' *Foreign Affairs*, vol. 42, April 1964, p. 462.

20  Ibid., p. 463.

21  H. R. P. Dickson, *The Arab and the Desert*, Allen & Unwin, London, 1949, p. 284.

22  Al Rashid, op. cit., p. 72.

23  H. R. P. Dickson, *The Arab and the Desert*, Allen & Unwin, London, 1949.

24  Amin Izz Aldin, *Ummal Al Kuwait Min Allulu Ela Al Petrol (Kuwaiti Workers: From Pearls to Petroleum)*, Government Printing Office, Kuwait, 1958, p. 4.

25  J. R. Wellsted, *Travel to the City of the Caliphs*, Henry Colburn, London, 1840, vol. 1, pp. 118–19.

26  Izz Aldin, op. cit., p. 5.

27  J. R. Wellsted, *Travel in Arabia*, John Murray, London, 1973, p. 267.

28  J. S. Buckingham, *Travel in Assyria, Medea and Persia*, Henry Colburn, London, 1829, p. 256.

29  M. Al Fara, *Al Tanmya Al Iqitasdya fe Dowlat Al Kuwait (Economic Development in Kuwait)*, Kuwait University, 1974, p. 69.

30  A. Villiers, *Son of Sinbad*, Scribners, New York, 1969.

31  For an interesting account of the various boats built in Kuwait see H. R. P. Dickson, *The Arab and the Desert*, Allen & Unwin, London 1949, ch. XXXVII, p. 473; see also Villiers, op. cit., p. 395.

32  Villiers, op. cit., pp. 398–9.

33  Fara, op. cit., p. 68.

34  A. Villiers, 'Some Aspects of the Arab Dhow Trade,' *Middle East Journal*, vol. 2, October 1948, p. 399.

35  Z. Freeth and V. Winstone, *Kuwait: Prospect and Reality*, Allen & Unwin, 1972.
36  Al Rumaihi, op. cit., p. 36.
37  A. Villiers, 'Some Aspects of the Arab Dhow Trade,' *Middle East Journal*, vol. 2, October 1948, p. 407.
38  Al Rashid, op. cit., p. 309.
39  I. Najjar, 'The Development of a One-Resource Economy: A Case Study of Kuwait', PhD thesis, Indiana University, 1969, p. 4.

## Notes to Chapter 2

1  A. H. T. Chisholm, *The First Kuwait Oil Concession: A Record of the Negotiations for the 1934 Agreement*, Frank Cass, London, 1975, p. 41.
2  IMF International Financial Statistics, April 1977, p. 442.
3  *The Middle East and North Africa 1976–77*, Europa, London, 1977, p. 472.
4  Stanford Research Institute and the American University, *Area Handbook for the Peripheral States of the Arabian Peninsula*, Government Printing, Washington DC, p. 117; also, I. Najjar, 'The Development of a One-Resource Economy: A Case Study of Kuwait', PhD thesis, Indiana University, 1969, p. 1.
5  Economic Intelligence Unit and the Planning Board of the Government of Kuwait, *Assessment of Joint Sector Operations in Kuwait*, vol. XVIII, Study Area 2, May 1974, p. 25.
6  Ibid.
7  UN Economic and Social Office in Beirut, *Studies on Selected Development Problems in Various Countries in the Middle East, 1967*, UN, New York, 1967, p. 32.
8  E. French and G. Hill, *Kuwait: Urban and Medical Ecology*, Springer, New York, 1971, p. 27.
9  Economic Intelligence Unit and the Planning Board of the Government of Kuwait, op. cit., p. 27.
10  UN Economic and Social Office in Beirut, *Studies on Selected Development Problems in Various Countries in the Middle East*, UN, New York, 1972, p. 59.
11  Ibid., p. 50.
12  French and Hill, op. cit., p. 29.
13  Frisendahl, 'Lecture Notes on Manpower Planning,' Kuwait Institute of Economic and Social Planning in the Middle East, April 1970, p. 2.
14  Government of Kuwait, Ministry of Planning, *The Five-Year Development Plan 1977–1981* (Population and Labor Force), p. 22 (Arabic).

15 Amiri Decree, No. 15, December 1959. See Hamad Al-Essa, *Al Majma Al Diema Lil Qawancen Al Kuwaitya (Collection of Kuwaiti Law)*, Al Resala Printing House, Kuwait.

16 See 'Nationality Law', in ibid.

17 A. Al Shamali, 'Manpower in Kuwait: Its Situation and Development.' Arab Planning Institute, Kuwait, 1971–2, p. 13.

18 J. Mouly and E. Costa, *Employment Policies in Less Developed Countries*, Allen & Unwin, London, 1974, p. 81.

19 Constitution of the State of Kuwait, November 11, 1972.

20 Chisholm, op. cit., p. 203.

21 Middle East Research and Information Project (MERP), no. 2, *Development in the Middle East.*

22 D. Finne, 'Recruitment and Training of Labor in the Middle East Oil Industry,' *Middle East Journal*, vol. 12, spring 1958, p. 141.

23 Ministry of Planning, *Annual Statistical Abstract 1976*, Government Printing, Kuwait, p. 329.

24 International Labour Office, *Manpower and Employment in Arab Countries: Some Critical Issues*, Beirut, May 1975, p. 17.

25 Ibid.

26 Edgar O. Edwards, *Employment in Developing Nations*, Report on a Ford Foundation Study, Columbia University Press, New York, 1974, p. 57.

27 Ali Sultan AlAli, 'Manpower Requirement in Kuwait,' paper presented to Kuwait Institute of Economic and Social Planning in the Middle East, June 1969, p. 26.

28 F. H. Harbison, 'Human Resources Development Planning in Modernizing Economies,' *International Labor Review*, May 1962, vol. 85, p. 437.

29 ILO, op. cit., p. 88.

30 F. H. Harbison and C. Myers, *Education, Manpower and Economic Growth*, McGraw-Hill, New York, 1964, p. 49.

31 C. A. Sinclair, 'General Education and Manpower Requirement in the Gulf States,' paper presented to the Bahrain Seminar on Human Resources Development in the Arabian Gulf, February 15–18, 1975, Bahrain.

32 UN Economic and Social Office in Beirut, *Studies on Selected Development Problems in Various Countries in the Middle East, 1967*, UN, New York, 1967, p. 11.

33 Sinclair, op. cit., p. 10.

## Notes to Chapter 3

1 M. S. Al Akhrass, 'The Labor Force Stability' (Arabic), Arab Planning Institute, Kuwait, 1976, p. 4.

2 Ministry of Planning, Central Statistical Office, *Annual Statistical Abstract 1976*, p. 31. See also Mahjub Mohammad, *Al Hijvah wal Altayeen Al Bonai Fe Almojtma Alkuwaiti (Migration and Structural Change in Kuwait Society)*, Nahdat Masev A Prenting, Cairo, 1970, p. 327.

3 Amin Izz Aldin, *Ummal al Kuwait, Min Allulu Ela al Petrol (Kuwaiti Workers: From Pearls to Petroleum)*, Government Printing Office, Kuwait, 1958, p. 15.

4 E. Long, *The Persian Gulf: An Introduction to Its Peoples, Politics and Economics*, Westview Press, Boulder, Colorado, 1976, p. 13.

5 W. R. Bohning and D. Maillat, *The Effects of the Employment of Foreign Workers*, OECD, Paris, 1974, p. 28.

6 D. Turnham, *The Employment in Less Developed Countries*, OECD Publication, Paris 1971, p. 11.

7 Al Nasrawi, *Financing Economic Development in Iraq*, Praeger, New York, 1967, p. 63.

8 S. Hadawi, *Bitter Harvest: Palestine Between 1914 and 1979*, Caravan Books, New York, 1979, p. 177.

9 *The New York Times*, Sunday, September 25, 1977, section 4, p. 2E.

10 International Labour Office, *Manpower and Employment in Arab Countries: Some Critical Issues*, Beirut, May 1975, p. 110.

11 Chase Manhattan Bank, *Middle East Markets*, June 23, 1975.

12 Republic of Iraq, Ministry of Planning, *Statistical Pocket Book*, 1974, p. 138.

13 *The Middle East and North Africa 1975–6*, Europa, London, 1977, p. 378.

14 Ferhang Jalal, *The Role of Government in the Industrialization of Iraq 1958–1965*. Frank Cass, London, 1972, p. 20.

15 E. Kanovsky, *Economic Development of Iraq*, David Horowitz Institute for Research of Developed Countries. Tel Aviv, 1974, paper no. 6, p. 39.

16 Al Nasrawi, op. cit., p. 63.

17 B. Shwadran, *The Middle East Oil and the Great Powers*, Wiley, New York, 1973, p. 92.

18 T. Y. Ismael, *Government and Politics of the Contemporary Middle East*, Dorsey Press, Homewood, Illinois, 1970, p. 162.

19 G. Lenozowski (ed.), *Political Elites in the Middle East*, American Enterprise Institute for Public Research, Washington, DC, 1975, p. 30.

20 M. S. Al Akhrass, *Population and Labor Force in Kuwait*, Arab Planning Institute, Kuwait, 1976, p. 78.

21 W. R. Bohning and D. Maillat, op. cit., p. 50.

22 Ibid., p. 11

*Notes*

23 Interview with Hamad Y. Alessa, former head of the Civil Service in Kuwait, Summer 1977.
24 Long. op. cit., p. 63.
25 Economic Intelligence Unit, *Middle East Annual Review 1977*, p. 216.
26 Ministry of Education, Census Department, *Census of Male and Female Teachers for the Years 1967-77*, Government Printing, Kuwait, p. 1.
27 Kuwait University, Information and Secretariat Department, *Statistics Academic Year 1975-76*, p. 69.
28 Stanford Research Institute, *Social and Economic Impacts of the Kuwait Government Compensation Increases of 1971-2 and Recommended National Compensation Policies*, Menlo Park, California, 1974, p. v-13.
29 M. S. Al Akhrass, *Madaher Estakrar Quat el Amel (Settlement of the Labor Force)*, Arab Planning Institute, Kuwait, 1976, p. 43.
30 International Bank for Reconstruction and Development, *The Economic Development of Kuwait*, Johns Hopkins Press, Baltimore, 1965, p. 61.
31 Stanford Research Institute, op. cit.
32 *Al Kuwait Al Youm* (government official publication), September 27, 1977, no. 1159.
33 *Al Qabas*, daily newspaper in Kuwait, Friday, January 23, 1976.
34 *Al Kuwait Al Youm* (government official publication), Sept. 19, 1977, no. 1157.
35 Ministry of Social Work and Labor, 'Qanun al Amel Fee Al Qata'eh el Ehli Qaqon No. 38 Issedin 1964' (Labor Law in the Private Sector, Law No. 38 for the Year 1964).
36 Willard A. Beling, *Pan Arabism and Labor*, Harvard Middle Eastern Monograph Series, Harvard University Press, 1961, p. 5.
37 Ahmad Al-Dean, 'Molahadat Hawel Tasad Al Harka Al Mutlabiya Li Tabaga Alummela' (The Increases of Working Class Demand), lecture delivered to Kuwait Confederation of Trade Unions, November 1974.
38 E. French and G. Hill, *Kuwait: Urban and Medical Ecology*, Springer, New York, 1971, p. 39.
39 Ibid. p. 39.
40 International Bank for Reconstruction and Development, op. cit., p. 9.
41 M. Field, *A Hundred Million Dollars a Day*, Sidgwick & Jackson, London, 1975, p. 83. Note that prior to independence in 1961, Kuwait used the Indian rupee as currency. In 1961 the currency was changed to the Kuwaiti Dinar.
42 A. Mackie, 'Social and Economic Tension Brings Kuwait Clampdown,' *Middle East Economic Digest*, September 1976.

43 *Al Anba*, Kuwaiti daily newspaper, Sunday, February 27, 1977.
44 *Middle East Economic Digest*, September 3, 1976.
45 *Kuwait Economist*, Kuwait Chamber of Commerce and Industry, no. 169, July 1977.
46 Ministry of Planning, *Annual Statistical Abstract 1976*, table 254.
47 *Middle East Economic Digest*, Annual Review, December 31, 1977.
48 See Article 17 of the 1964 law in Alessa, *Al Majmua'h Addaeeman Lel Qawneen el Kuwateeah (The Permanent Collection of Kuwaiti Law)*, Al Resala Printing House, Kuwait, vol. 5.
49 For example, M. Sani, M. DaZera and M. SiRamadan, 'A Field Study of Kuwait Cooperatives,' *Journal of Social Science*, no. 2, October 1974, Kuwait University, p. 31.
50 Interview with Salam Al Sabah, Minister of Social Affairs and Labor, *Alwatan* (Daily Newspaper), May 14, 1977.
51 Stanford Research Institute, op. cit., pp. 1–13.
52 Stanford Research Institute and the American University of Washington, *Area Handbook for the Peripheral States of the Arabian Peninsula*, Government Printing, Washington DC, p. 102.
53 *Alwatan* (Kuwaiti daily newspaper), October 5, 1977.
54 Long, op. cit., p. 30.
55 H. A. Al Ebraheem, *Kuwait: A Political Study*, Kuwait University, 1975, p. 121.
56 International Bank for Reconstruction and Development, op. cit., p. 24.
57 Al Ebraheem, op. cit., p. 122.
58 A. Inkeles and D. Smith, *Becoming Modern: Individual Change in Six Developing Countries*, Harvard University Press, Cambridge, Mass., 1974, p. 15.
59 D. Lerner, *The Passing of Traditional Society*, Free Press, New York, 1958, p. 60.
60 French and Hill, op. cit., p. 00.
61 S. E. M. Ibrahim, 'Overurbanization and Underurbanism: the case of the Arab World,' *International Journal of the Middle East*, vol. 6, January 1975, p. 40.
62 M. Halpern, *The Politics of Social Change in the Middle East and North Africa*, Princeton University Press, 1963, p. 52.
63 T. Y. Ismael, *The Arab Left*, Syracuse University Press, 1976, p. 99.
64 Economic Intelligence Unit, op. cit., p. 212.
65 H. Al Kajal, *Tarik Al Kuwait Al Siyasi (Kuwait Political History)*, Dar Al Kutub, Beirut, vol. 2, p. 258.
66 N. H. Aruri, 'Kuwait: A Political Study,' *Muslim World*, vol. 60, October 1970, p. 321.
67 Economic Intelligence Unit and the Planning Board of the Government of Kuwait, 'Assessment of Joint Sector Operations in Kuwait,' vol. XVIII, Area 2, May 1974, p. 45.

*Notes*

68 *Middle East Economic Digest*, June 18, 1976.
69 *Al Anba* (Kuwaiti newspaper), March 27, 1976.
70 Stanford Research Institute, *Social and Economic Impact of the Kuwaiti Government Compensation Increases of 1971-2 and Recommended National Compensation Policies*, Menlo Park, California, 1974, pp. v–24.
71 *Al Watan* (Kuwaiti daily newspaper), September 22, 1977.

## Notes to Chapter 4

1 W. Schultz, 'Capital Formation by Education,' *Journal of Political Economy*, 68, December 1960, no. 6, p. 571.
2 G. S. Becker, 'Investment in Human Capital: A Theoretical Analysis,' *Journal of Political Economy*, 70, October 1962, p. 9.
3 F. H. Harbison, 'Human Resources Development Planning in Modernising Economies,' *International Labor Review*, 85, May 1962, p. 438.
4 A. Curle, 'Some Aspects of Educational Planning in Underdeveloped Countries,' *Harvard Educational Review*, 32, Summer 1962, no. 3, p. 292.
5 USAID/NEC, 'Far East Manpower Assessment and Educational Planning Seminar', Manila, February 12–17, 1965, p. 1.
6 Ministry of Planning, *First Five-Year Development Plan: 1967–8, to 1971–2*, Kuwait, December 1968, p. 63.
7 A. A. Al Rashid, *Tarik al Kuwait (History of Kuwait)*, Dar al Hayat, Beirut, 1971, p. 373.
8 M. Al-Muhanini, Descriptive Study of Public Education in Kuwait, PhD thesis, George Washington University, 1974, p. 21.
9 *Al-Watan* (Kuwaiti daily newspaper), June 16, 1977.
10 Ministry of Education, Statistics Department, 'Report Submitted to the Educational Seminar in Geneva, September 1977,' p. 39.
11 Ministry of Planning, *Annual Statistical Abstract 1979*, table 294, p. 334.
12 Qanon no. 11 of 1965, related to compulsory education.
13 Planning Board, Social Planning Division, *Educational Service Sector in the Five-Year Plan, 1976/7 1980/1*, 1975, p. 15.
14 J. A. Socknat (Ford Foundation), 'An Inventory and Assessment of Employment-Oriented Human Resources Development Program in ‑the Gulf Area', Bahrain Conference on Human Resources in the Gulf, February 1975.
15 Harbison, op. cit., p. 437.
16 C. A. Sinclair, General Education and Manpower Requirements in the Gulf States, paper delivered at the Bahrain Seminar on

Human Resources Development in the Arabian Gulf, Bahrain, February 1975, p. 12.

17  D. K. Wheeler, 'Educational Problems of Arab Countries,' *International Review of Education*, XII, no. 1, 1966, p. 313.

18  F. Harbison and I. Ibrahim, *Human Resources for Egyptian Enterprise*, McGraw-Hill, New York, 1968, p. 106.

19  Ministry of Education, Statistics Department, *General Statistics, no. 3*.

20  Amin Izz Aldin, *Ummal al Kuwait Min Allulu Ela al Petrol (Kuwaiti Workers: from Pearls to Petroleum)*, Government Printing Office, Kuwait, 1958, p. 29.

21  Ministry of Social Affairs and Labor, *Annual Report 1955*.

22  R. Patai, *The Arab Mind*, Scribner, New York, 1976, p. 115.

23  Council of Ministers, Central Vocational Training Directorate, 'Assessment of the Training Potentials in the Government Sector' (Arabic), April 1973, p. 10.

24  Harbison, op. cit., p. 451.

25  Socknat, op. cit.

26  M. G. Rumaihi, 'Human Capital in the Gulf: A Way for Lasting Development,' paper presented at the Association of Arab American University Graduates in Kuwait, December 1975.

27  Ministry of Social Affairs and Labor, Manpower Division, 'A Report and Follow-up on Graduates of Vocational Training Centers' (Arabic), 1974.

28  L. Sharaff, *Training Programs for Manpower Development in the Oil Companies in Kuwait*, Arab Planning Institute, Kuwait, 1972, p. 36.

29  Sinclair, op. cit.

30  E. O. Edwards, *Employment in Developing Countries*, Columbia University Press, New York, 1974, p. 316.

## Notes to Chapter 5

1  F. Harbison and C. Myers, *Education, Manpower and Economic Growth*, McGraw-Hill, New York, 1964, p. 52.

2  M. A. Qali, 'Occupational Adjustment among Workers in Kuwait' (Arabic), *Faculty of Arts and Education Bulletin*, Kuwait University, No. 5, June 1974, p. 158.

3  A. M. Lorenzo, *Lecture Notes on Manpower Planning*, Kuwait Institute of Economic and Social Planning in the Middle East, April 1970, p. 9.

4  Asker, 'Over-Employment in the Government Sector' (Arabic), Seminar on high-level management, Kuwait, January 16–19, 1977, Kuwait Arab Institute, p. 9.

*Notes*

Y. Al Hamad, Head of KRAD, *International Development Review*, 1975, no. 3.

6 The left in Kuwait is associated with the Arab Nationalist Movement. Since 1967, it has been associated with the Popular Front for the Liberation of Palestine, a Marxist-orientated movement within the Palestine Liberation Organization.

7 Stanford Research Institute, *Social and Economic Impact of the Kuwaiti Government Compensation Increases of 1971-2 and Recommended National Compensation Policies*, Menlo Park, California, 1974, p. vi-4.

8 *The Economist*, March 20, 1976, p. 107.

9 *Al Taliah* (Kuwaiti weekly newspaper), May 4, 1974.

10 Stanford Research Institute, op. cit., pp. vii-2.

11 *Kuwait*, Permanent Mission of the State of Kuwait to the UN, vol. XII, no. 2, February 1975.

12 USAID/NEC, 'Fareast Manpower Assessment and Educational Planning Seminar.' Manila, February 12-17, 1965, p. 1.

13 G. Myrdal, *Asian Drama: An Inquiry into the Poverty of Nations*, Pantheon, New York, 1968, vol. III, ch. 31, p. 1622.

14 G. Aded, Planning for High Level Manpower in the Arab World, paper delivered at the Arab American Graduate Association Conference in Kuwait, December 28-31, 1975.

15 M. Reda, 'The New Trend in Education,' lecture delivered to Kuwait General Conference on School Curriculum, Kuwait, March 1972.

16 S. M. Lipset and Solari, *Elites in Latin America*, Oxford University Press, 1967, p. 45.

17 Harbison and Mayer, op. cit., p. 68.

18 F. Harbison and I. A. Ibrahim, *Human Resources for Egyptian Enterprise*, McGraw-Hill, New York, 1958, p. 106.

19 K. Wheeler, 'Education Problems of Arab Countries,' *International Review of Education*, vol. XII, no. 1, 1966, p. 313.

20 SRI, op. cit.

21 Interview with Dr Ali Abdul Raheem, Dean of the Business School at Kuwait University; *Al Watan* (Kuwaiti daily newspaper), September 25, 1977.

22 al Qina, *Safahat Min Tarik al Kuwait (Short History of Kuwait)*, Government Printing Office, Kuwait, 1968.

23 D. C. Gordon, *Women of Algeria: An Essay on Change*, Harvard University Press, 1968, p. 9.

24 Family Development Society, *March of the Kuwaiti Women in 11 Years Through the Family Development Society*, Kuwait, 1974, p. 108.

25 There are two women's associations in Kuwait founded 1962-3: the Family Development Society and the Women's Cultural Society.

126

26  Family Development Society, op. cit., p. 109.

27  N. H. Yousseff, 'Differential Labor Force Participation of Women in Latin American and Middle Eastern Countries: The Influence of Family Characteristics,' *Social Forces*, December 1972, vol. 51, no. 2, p. 145.

28  Speech delivered by the Amir of Kuwait, Shaikh Sabah Al Salem Al Sabah, on the occasion of 'Women's Day' in Kuwait, 1970. In N. Al Sadani, *History of Kuwaiti Women*, Dar Al Syasa, Kuwait, 1974.

29  Gordon, op. cit., p. 46.

30  F. Mernissi, *Beyond the Veil: Male and Female Dynamics in a Modern Muslim Society*, Wiley, New York, 1975, p. xv.

31  J. J. Terry, 'Working Women in Arab Nations,' paper delivered at the Association of Arab-American University Graduates, Tenth Annual Convention, Detroit, Michigan, October 21–23.

32  Al Senbany, 'Women's Education and Its Relation to the Labor Force in the Arab World,' paper delivered at the Association of Arab-American University Graduates Conference in Kuwait, December 1975.

33  Amir Decree, Nationality Law, No. 15, 1959.

34  Izz Al Din Abdulla, 'Tashreah Al Jenseah Al Kuwateeah' (Kuwaiti Nationality Law), *L'Egypte contemporaine*, July 1975, Issue No. 361, Cairo.

35  F. Stoakes, 'Social and Political Changes in the Third World' in D. Hopwook (ed.), *The Arabian Peninsula: Society and Politics*, Allen & Unwin, London, 1972, p. 203.

36  *New York Times*, February 19, 1978.

37  Ibid.

# Bibliography

Abdu Mohammad, *Al Hezra Wal Ta Tower Al Beani Fe Al Majtama Al Kuwaiti* (Immigration & Population Structural Change), Arabic, Cairo, Egypt, Nahdat Masser Publication, 1977.

Abdulla, Saif Abbas, 'Politics Administration & Urban Planning in Welfare Society: Kuwait,' PhD thesis, Indiana University, 1973.

Aimohani, Mohammad, *A Descriptive Study of Public Education in Kuwait*, PhD thesis, George Washington University, Ed.D. 1974.

Al Ebraheem, Hassan A., *Kuwait: A Political Study*, Kuwait University, 1975.

Al Qinai, Yousif Ben Essa, *Safahat Min Tarik al Kuwait* (Short History of Kuwait), Arabic, Government Printing Office, Kuwait, 1968.

Al Rashaed, Abdulaziz, *Tarik al Kuwait* (History of Kuwait), Arabic, Dar al Hayat, Beirut, Lebanon, 1971.

Al Rumaihi, Mohammad, *Al Petrol Wal Tatawer al Ijtimai fe al Kalez al Arabi* (Oil & Social Change in the Arabian Gulf), Arabic, Dar Al Shaeb, Cairo, Egypt, 1975.

Al Sabah, Yousif al Fadel, 'Economic Transformation of Kuwait: A Study of Dualistic Economy with Capital Surplus,' PhD thesis, Fletcher School of Law & Diplomacy, 1970.

Al Sarawi, Abdul Aziz, *Derasat Fe Al Shown Al Ijtimaya Wal Ummal* (Studies of Social Affairs & Labor), Arabic, Government Printing Office, 1965.

Al Sarawi, Abdul Aziz, *Al Tashriat Al Ijtimaya Fe Al Kuwait* (The Legal Aspect of Social Affairs in Kuwait), Arabic, Kuwait Government Printing Office, 1968.

Al Sharnobi, Mohammad, *Al Tarkib Al Sokarsi fee Dowlat Al Kuwait* (The Population Structure in the State of Kuwait), Arabic, Anglo-Egyptian Print, Cairo, Egypt, 1971.

Anthony, John Duke (ed.), *The Middle East: Oil, Politics and Development*, American Enterprise Institute, Washington, DC, 1975.

Arab Planning Institute (Kuwait), and the Government of the State of Bahrain, *Seminar on Human Resources Development in the Arabian Gulf*, Bahrain, 15–18 February 1975.

Arab-American University Graduate and Kuwait National Council for Culture, Arts & Letters, *Conference on Issues in Human Resources Development in the Arab World*, 28–31 December, 1975.

Belling, Willard A., *Pan Arabism and Labor*, Harvard University Press, Cam., Mass., 1961.

Bohning, W. R. and Maillat, D., *The Effects of the Employment of Foreign Workers*, OECD Publication, Paris, 1974.

Bo Bramsen, Michele and Tinker, Irene, *Women and World Development*, Overseas Development Council, Paris, 1976.

Buckingham, J. S., *Travels in Assyria, Medea and Persia*, Henry Colburn, London, 1829.

Cook, David C., *Kuwait: Miracle on the Desert*, Grosset & Dunlap, New York, 1970.

Cooper, Charles (ed.), *Economic Development and Population Growth in the Middle East*, American Elsevier, NY, 1972.

Dickson, H. R. P., *The Arab of the Desert*, Allen & Unwin, London, 1949.

Dickson, H. R. P., *Kuwait and Her Neighbours*, Allen & Unwin, London, 1956.

Edwards, Edgar O., *Employment in Developing Nations*, Report on a Ford Foundation Study, Columbia University Press, NY, 1974.

El Sheikh Riad, Kuwait, *Economic Growth of the Oil State: Problems & Politicies*, publication of Kuwait University, 1972-3.

French, G. E. and Hill, Allan, *Kuwait: Urban and Medical Ecology*, Springer Verlag, Berlin, 1971.

Halpen, Manfred, *The Politics of Social Change in the Middle East and North Africa*, Princeton University Press, NJ, 1966.

Harbison, F. and Myers, *Education, Manpower and Economic Growth*, McGraw-Hill, New York, 1964.

Harbison, F. and Myers, *Manpower and Education*, McGraw-Hill, New York, 1965.

Harbison, F. and Ibrahim Abdel Kader, *Human Resources for Egyptian Enterprise*, McGraw-Hill, New York, 1958.

Hopwood, Derk (ed.), *The Arabian Peninsula: Society and Politics*, Allen & Unwin, London, 1972.

ILO, *Manpower and Employment in Arab Countries: Some Critical Issues*, International Labor Office, Geneva, 1975.

Izz Aldin Amin, *Ummal Al Kuwait Min Al Lulu Ela Al Petrol* (Kuwait Workers: From Pearl Diving to Petroleum), Kuwait, Government Printing Office, 1958.

Kaysa, Bernard, *Manpower Movements and Labor Migration*, OECD Publication, Paris, 1971

Bibliography

Locker, Robert D., *Manpower Development in Africa*, Praeger, New York, 1969.

Long, David, *The Persian Gulf: An Introduction to its People, Politics, and Economics*, Westview Press, Boulder, Colorado, 1976.

Mernissi, Fatima, *Beyond the Veil: Male-Female Dynamics in Modern Muslum Society*, Wiley, New York, 1975.

Mertz, Robert Anton, *Education and Manpower in the Arabian Gulf*, American Friends of the Middle East, 1972.

Millen, Bruce H., *The Political Role of Labor in Developing Countries*, Brookings Institute, Washington, DC, 1963.

Myrdal, Gunnar, *Asian Drama: An Inquiry into the Poverty of Nations*, Pantheon, New York, 1968.

Peacock, Alan and Hauser, Gerald, *Government Finance and Economic Development*, OECD Publication, Paris, 1975.

Planning Board, Bureau of Census, *The Population Census 1975*, Arabic, 2 vols, Government Printing Press, Kuwait.

Planning Board, Bureau of Census, *The Census of Government Employees 1972*, Arabic, Government Printing Press, Kuwait.

Planning Board, Bureau of Census, *Report on Employment, Wages & Hours of Work for the Years 1967, 68 & 69*, Arabic, Government Printing Press, Kuwait.

Planning Board, *Kuwait Economy in 1968, 69: A Survey*, Government Printing Press, Kuwait.

Planning Board, *Al Iqtisad Al Kuwaiti 1970-72* (Kuwait Economy 1970-2), Government Printing Press, Kuwait.

Planning Board, *Estimate of the Manpower Supply & Demand Between 1975-80*, Arabic, Government Printing Press, Kuwait.

Planning Board, *Census of the Public Service Sector 1973*, Arabic, Government Printing Press, Kuwait.

Planning Board, *Annual Statistical Abstract, 1974*, Government Printing Press, Kuwait.

Planning Board, *Annual Statistical Abstract, 1975*, Government Printing Press, Kuwait.

Shiber, Saba George, *Kuwait the Unique: A Collection of Articles*, Kuwait, April 1961.

Stanford Research Institute, *Social and Economic Impacts of the Kuwaiti Government Compensation Increases of 1971-72 and Recommended National Policy*, Menlo Park, Calif., 1974.

SRI and American University, *Area Handbook for the Peripheral State of the Arabian Peninsula*, Government Printing Office, Washington, DC.

Szyliowics, Joseph S., *Education and Modernization in the Middle East*, Cornell University Press, NY, 1973.

Trebous, Madeleine, *Migration and Development*, OECD Publication, Paris, 1970.

Turnham, David, *The Employment Problem in Less Developed Countries*, OECD Publication, Paris, 1971.

United Nations, Economic and Social Office in Beirut, *Studies on Selected Development Problems in Various Countries in the Middle East 1967*, UN, New York, 1967.

United Nations, *Studies on Selected Development Problems in Various Countries in the Middle East 1968*, UN, New York, 1968.

United Nations, *Studies on Selected Development Problems in Various Countries in the Middle East 1969*, UN, New York, 1969.

United Nations, *Studies on Selected Development Problems in Various Countries in the Middle East 1970*, UN, New York, 1970.

United Nations, *Studies on Selected Development Problems in Various Countries in the Middle East 1971*, UN, New York, 1971.

United Nations, *Studies on Selected Development Problems in Various Countries in the Middle East 1972*, UN, New York, 1972.

## Papers and Periodicals

A Sayigh Yousif, 'Under Employment: Concept and Measurement,' *Middle East Economic Paper-Economic Research Institute American University of Beirut*, 1956.

A Sayigh Yousif, 'Management-Labor Relations in Selected Arab Countries: Major Aspects and Determinations', *International Labor Review*, vol. 77, June 1958.

A Sayigh Yousif, 'Dilemas of Arab Management,' *Middle East Economic Paper, Economic Research Institute American University of Beirut*, 1960.

A Sayigh Yousif, 'Problems and Prospects of Development in the Arabian Peninsula,' *International Journal of the Middle East Studies*, vol. 2, no. 1, January 1971.

Al Shamali Abdulhameed A., 'Manpower in Kuwait: Its Situation and Development,' The Arab Planning Institute, Kuwait, 1971-2.

Aruri Naseer H., 'Kuwait: A Political Study,' *The Muslim World*, vol. 60, October 1970.

Becker, Gary S., 'Investment in Human Capital: A Theoretical Analysis,' *The Journal of Political Economy*, October 1962, vol. 70.

Calverley, Edward E., 'Kuwait Today, Yesterday and Tomorrow,' *The Muslim World*, vol. 52, January 1962.

Candole, E. A., 'Developments in Kuwait,' *Royal Central Asian Society Journal*, vol. 42, 1955.

Curle, Adam, 'Some Aspects of Educational Planning in Underdeveloped Areas', *Harvard Educational Review*, no. 2, Summer 1962.

Dobson, Meric, 'Labor in Kuwait.' *Middle East Forum*, vol. 39, 1963.

Economic Intelligence Unit and The Planning Board of the Government of Kuwait, 'Assessment of Joint Sector Operations in Kuwait, vol. 18, Study Area 2', May 1974.

EIU, *Spending Oil Revenues: Development Prospects in the Middle East to 1975.*

Finne, David, 'Recruitment and Training of Labor the Middle East Oil Industry,' *Middle East Journal*, vol. 12, no. 2, Spring 1958.

Harbison, F., 'Human Resources Development Planning in Modernizing Economies,' *International Labor Review*, vol. 85, May 1962.

Harbison, F. *et al.*, 'The Labor Problem in Economic Development,' *International Labor Review*, vol. 71, January–June 1955.

Hay, Rupert, 'The Impact of the Oil Industry on the Persial Gulf Shaykhdoms.' *Middle East Journal*, vol. 9, no. 4, Autumn 1955.

Heard Bey Franke, 'The Gulf States & Oman in Transition,' *Asian Affairs*, vol. 59, pt. 1, February 1972.

Kergan, J. L., 'Social & Economic Changes in the Gulf Countries.' *Asian Affairs*, vol. 62, October 1975.

Langley, S. J., 'Oil Royalties and Economic Development,' *Middle East Economic Paper*, American University of Beirut, 1954.

Monroe, Elizabeth, 'The Shaikhdom of Kuwait.' *International Affairs* vol. 30, no. 3, July 1954.

Paul Balfour, H. G., 'Recent Developments in the Persian Gulf.' *Journal of the Royal Central Asian Society*, vol. 56, February 1968.

Pelly, Lewis, 'Remarks on the Tribes, Trade & Resources Around the Shoreline of the Persian Gulf.' *Transactions of the Bombay Geographical Society*, vol. 17, January 1863–December 1864.

Sara, Nathir G., 'Problems of Educational Research in the Middle East,' *International Review of Education*, vol. 21, 1975.

Schultz, Theordore W., 'Capital Formation by Education,' *Journal of Political Economy*, vol. 68, no. 6, December 1960.

Schultz, Theodore W., 'Reflections on Investment in Man,' *The Journal of Political Economy*, vol. 70, Supplement: no. 5, pt. 2, October 1962.

Shehab, Fakhri, 'Kuwait: A Super Affluent Society,' *Foreign Affairs*, vol. 42, April 1964.

Sinclair, C. A. and Brisks, J. S., *International Migration Project Country Case Study: Kuwait (Part One)*, University of Durham, Department of Economics, England, 1977.

Stork, Joe, 'Oil Revenues and Industrialization,' *Development in the Middle East, MERIP Reports* (Middle East Research and Information Project), no. 42.

Terry, Janice, 'Working Women in Arab Nations.' papers delivered at the Arab-American University Graduation held in Detroit, 20 October 1977.

Villiers, Alan, 'Some Aspects of the Arab Dhow Trade,' *Middle East Journal*, vol. 2, October 1948.

Youssef, Nadia, 'Differential Labor Force Participation of Women in Latin America & the Middle Eastern Countries: The Influence of Family Characteristics,' *Social Forces*, vol. 51, no. 2, December 1972.

## Arab Planning Institute Studies

Al Ali Ali Sultan, *Manpower Requirement in Kuwait*, The Arab Planning Institute, Kuwait, 1969.

Al Akhrass, M. S., *Population and Labor Force in Kuwait*, Arabic, The Arab Planning Instutute, Kuwait, 1976.

Boyath, Mohammed, *Iranian Manpower in Kuwait: Study of Mobility in Jobs*, Arabic, The Arab Planning Institute, Kuwait, 1974–75.

Frisendahl, Harald (ILO Adviser), *Lecture Notes on Manpower Planning*, The Arab Planning Institute, Kuwait, April 1970.

LoRenzo, A. M. (ILO Adviser), *Lecture Notes on Manpower Planning*, The Arab Planning Institute, Kuwait, April 1970.

Saraff, Lila, *Training Programmes for Manpower Development in the Oil Companies in Kuwait*, The Arab Planning Institute, Kuwait, 1971–2.

Shyjah, Abbas Khudhayir, *Iraqi Manpower in Kuwait*, The Arab Planning Institute, Kuwait, May 1968.

Yasin, Mohammad (ILO expert), *Administration Structure for Manpower Planning in Kuwait*, The Arab Planning Institute, Kuwait, April 1974.

Yasin, Mohammad (ILO expert), *Manpower Resources Requirements and Problems of Kuwait*, Planning Board, State of Kuwait, October 1974.

# Index

accountancy, 23
administration, employment in, 22, 24–5, 51; *see also* civil service; government
adult education, 85, 97
affluence, 15, 29, 54, 116; *see also* economic factors; income
Africa, 4, 7, 18, 117
age of population, xiv, 12–15, 88, 114
Agricultural Institute, 74, 76
agriculture, 33, 36–8, 41
Ajman tribe, 2
Al Khatib, Dr Ahmad, 54
Al Sabah family, 1
Al Sabah, Shaikh Ahmed Al Jaber, 3
Al Sabah, Shaikh Mubarak, 2, 54, 56
Al Thakeb, Fahad, 101
Alkafala system, 45
American Independent Oil Co., 79–80
Anaizz tribe, 1
Anglo-Iranian Oil Co., 38
Anglo-Persian Oil Co., 10
APOC *see* Anglo-Persian
Arab Ba'ath Socialist Party, 53
Arab loyalties, 1–3
Arab Nationalist movement, 53–4, 123
Arab Planning Institute, 63, 66, 78, 111, 113
Arabian Oil Co., 79–80

Arab-Israeli War, 34
arts education, 68, 96

Badu people, 83
Baggala, 7
Bahrain, 8–9
Becker, G. S., 56, 122
Bedouins, 2, 108–9, 115
Belem, 7
Beni Khalid tribe, 1
Bint al Amm, 8
birth rate 15, 29; *see also* population
boat-building, 7–8
bonus salary, 24, 60; *see also* income
bureaucratization, 52–3, 55, 89–94; *see also* civil service
Business Institute, 97

Canada Dry Co., 46
Canada, 71, 109
Central Vocational Training Directorate, 74–6, 111; *see also* education, vocational
children, numbers of 12, 14–15, 88, 114; *see also* education
Civil Service, 75, 98–94, 111, 113; *see also* administration; bureaucratization
Civil Aviation Institute, 74
class *see* manual labour; middle class
Commercial School 73

commerce: education in, 63, 68, 73; employment in, 19–20
construction industry, 19–20
Consultative Council, 3
contracts, 45
co-operatives, 50, 121
cost: of education, 60, 66, 76–7, 98; of housing, 41, 44, 48–9; of goods, 32, 49
currency, 120

development *see* economic development; reform
discrimination: against immigrants, 44–50, 55, 60, 106; against women, 16–18, 27, 101–6; *see also* social barriers
doctors *see* health workers

Eastern and General Syndicate, 10
economic development, xiii–xiv, 3–9, 18–19, 50, 56–7, 93–4, 119; *see also* industry; oil industry
economic factors: in immigration, 32–3, 36, 38; in manpower planning, 103; *see also* affluence
economic treaties, 3
economics, 23, 63, 68
education: abroad, 62–3, 66–7, 71, 77, 81, 86, 105; adult, 85, 97; of civil servants, 89–90; and class, 53; costs of, 60, 66, 76–7, 98; development of, 57–60, 63, 87; and discrimination, 60; dropouts, 63, 97; and economic development, 56–7; free, 32, 60; higher, 9, 24, 27–8, 63–9, 71, 86, 91–2, 96–7, 110, 113; immigrant, 15, 24, 27, 36, 43–4, 48–51, 57–62, 67–71, 81, 85, 96, 110–11; and incentives, 71–2; and manpower, 63–87; level of, 9, 27–9; on-the-job, 75–6; reform of, xiv, 95–9, 122, 124; and socialization, 51; vocational and technical, 65–8, 71–81, 97–9, 105, 111, 123; and women, 27, 57, 60, 63–71,
74, 105–6, 125; *see also* illiteracy; Ministry of Education; teachers
*Education, Manpower and Economic Growth*, 90
EGS *see* Eastern and General Syndicate
Egypt/Egyptian: education, 50, 57, 59, 61, 67, 70–1, 77, 105; manpower, 32, 35–6, 39–43, 50–1, 57, 59, 70; women, 36
Egyptian Code, 51
emigration, 55, 109
Employer Association, 112
employment *see* labor force; manpower; occupations
engineering, 23, 66, 68, 74, 76
England *see* United Kingdom
Europe, Western: education in, 62–3, 67, 71, 81; emigration to, 109; manpower from, 39–42, 80

Family Development Society, 124
Fatah, 41
Fire Brigade School, 74
Five-Year Development Plan, 117
foreign manpower in Kuwait, 31–55; *see also* immigrants
France, and education, 62–3, 67, 69, 71, 96
freedom of speech and press, 33

Gaza Strip, 34
geography of Kuwait, 1
Ghowass, 6
Gibb, H. A. R., 101
gold, 7
Gordon, D., 104, 124
government: and education abroad, 63, 66–7; as employer, 18–19, 22–4, 29, 83, 88–94, 123; and housing, 47–9; immigrants in, 41, 51; *see also* civil service; Ministry
graduates, 24, 27–8, 86, 91–2; *see also* education, higher; Kuwait University
Great Britain *see* United Kingdom

Gross National Products, 16, 36;
see also economic development
growth of population, 11–16, 29,
51–2, 114
Gulf Oil Co., 10
Gulf states: manpower from, 31,
33, 40, 109; students from, 61,
68; trade with, 3

Halpern, M., 53, 121
Harbison, F. H., 24–5, 56, 90,
118, 122–4
health education, 105
health facilities, 15; see also
social services
Health Occupatons and Training
Institute, 74
health workers, 23, 36, 50, 66,
74, 76, 105
higher education see education
history of Kuwait, 1–9, 115, 117
Holland, 71
Holmes, Major, 10
housing, 41, 44, 47–9

Ibrahim, S. E. M., 52, 121
illegal immigrants, 32, 43
illiteracy, xiv, 27–8, 44, 83–4,
88–90, 97, 104–5; see also
education
immigrants: age of, 12, 14–15;
discrimination against, 44–50,
55, 60, 106; in government,
41, 51; illegal, 32, 43; incentives
for, 41, 44, 69; labor force,
16–55; legal and economic
conditions of, 43–50; numbers
of, xiv, 11–13; professional,
36, 41, 50; profile of, 39–43;
pull factor, 31–3; push factor,
33–9; uncertainty in, 50–4;
women, 16–17, 34–6, 39, 60;
see also education; manpower
immigration: mass, fear of, 109;
reasons for, 31–9
imports, 11–12; see also trade
incentives, 41, 44, 69, 71–2
income: civil service, 92; equitable,
19; high, 11, 31, 35, 41, 44;
oil, 11–12; teachers', 24, 60;

from trade, 4–8; unequal, 49,
55; see also affluence; economic factors
India, 1, 51; manpower from,
32–3, 39–40, 42, 51, 80;
trade with, 4, 7
Industrial Bank, 94
Industrial College, 72–3, 75
industry, 19–20, 73–87, 93–4;
see also economic development;
oil industry
inflation, 48–9; see also costs
Inkeles, A., 52, 121
Institute for Applied Engineering,
74, 76
Institute of Nursing, 74
International Bank, 44, 113,
120–1
International Development,
Agency for, 113
International Labor Office, 25,
118–19
International Labor Organization,
113
investments, 93–4
Iran/Iranian, 1; manpower, 31–4,
36, 38–42, 109; women, 39
Iraq/Iraqui, 1, 119; agriculture,
36–7; education, 59, 61, 67,
70; manpower, 31–4, 36–43,
51; trade, 4, 7
Islam, 1, 8, 40, 46, 57, 101–2,
104
Israel, 2

Jordan/Jordanian: education, 59,
61, 70, 105; manpower, 34–5,
39–42, 51
judicial system see legal system

Kafeel system, 44–5
Kinko, 46
kinship, 103; see also tribes
KNPC see Kuwait National
Petroleum Co.
KOC see Kuwait Oil Co.
Kuwait: education and man-
power in, 56–87; foreign
manpower in, 31–55; history
of, 1–9, 115; manpower in,

10–30; manpower planning in, 88–114; people of, 1–3
Kuwait-Arab Planning Institute, 63, 66, 78, 111, 113, 117
Kuwait Lawyers Association, 49
Kuwait National Petroleum Co., 79–81
Kuwait Oil Co., 79–81
Kuwait Shell Oil Co., 79
Kuwait Spanish Oil Co., 79–80
Kuwait University, 63, 66–8, 71, 86, 93, 96–7, 110, 113, 119, 124; *see also* education, higher
Kuwaiti Trade union, 46
Kuwaitization, 23–4, 91

labor force, 16–29, 119, 122; failings of, 89–90; numbers of, 88–9, 107; *see also* manpower
Labor Law, 46
Labor Office, 32
land policy, 47–8
law *see* legal system
Lebanon/Lebanese: education, 59, 61, 67, 70; manpower, 34–5, 40, 42–3
legal and economic conditions of immigrants, 43–50
legal system, 23, 49, 51, 63, 68, 96, 115
legislation against women, 16–17
Lerner, Daniel, 52, 121
Libya, 55
Lipset, S. M., 96, 124
living standards *see* affluence; income
Lorimer, 3

Manpower Center, 111–14
manpower: defined, 16; and education, 63–87; planning, xiii–xiv, 88–114, 117–18; *see also* immigrants; labor force
manual labor, 5–7, 52; attitudes to, xiv, 2, 20, 29, 71–2, 75; skilled, 7, 9, 26, 41, 71–81, 83; unskilled, 34, 43–4, 49; *see also* labor force; manpower
manufacturing *see* industry

marriage, 8, 15, 43, 102
merchant class, 3
Mernissi, F., 104, 124
middle class, 3, 49, 52–4, 94
Middle East Research and Information Project, 118
Ministry *see* government
Ministry of Communication, 74
Ministry of Defense, 71, 74
Ministry of Education, 43, 48, 60–3, 67, 70, 72–3, 97, 113, 119; *see also* education
Ministry of Electricity and Water, 74
Ministry of Health, 74, 76
Ministry of Information, 76
Ministry of Interior, 45, 108, 111, 113
Ministry of Justice, 49
Ministry of Planning, 67, 75, 84–5, 106, 111, 113, 117–18, 120
Ministry of Public Works, 74, 76
Ministry of Social Affairs and Labor, 32, 72, 74, 77, 111, 113, 120, 123
Ministry of Trade and Industry, 76
modernization, 52–5
Mossedegh, Dr Muhammad, 38
multinationals, 98
Muslim *see* Islam
Myers, C., 25, 90, 118, 123
Myrdal, G., 95, 124

Nasser, President, 53–4
National Assembly, 93–4, 108; Election Law, 103–4
Nationality Law, reform of, 106–11, 114, 125
nationalization of oil industry, 94
Naukhada, 5–6
Negro workers, 8
*New York Times*, 34, 110, 124
non-Kuwaiti population *see* immigrants
nursing *see* health workers

occupations, 29, 41–4, 49, 81–2; *see also* labor force; manpower; manual labor

oil industry: companies, 10, 38,
79–80; Concession, 20; discovery of oil, 10–11, 117;
employment in, 19–21, 29;
nationalization of, 94; occupations in, 81–2; and population increase, 51–2; refining,
20–1; revenue from, 11–12;
and social composition, 52–3,
115; vocational training in,
79–81; and women's liberation,
99; *see also* industry
Oman, manpower from 9, 31, 33,
36, 39–40
on-the-job training, 75–6
open-door policy, 31–2
opportunity, lack of *see* discrimination
overpopulation, 35; *see also*
population

Pakistan: education in, 67;
manpower from, 33, 39–40,
42, 80
Palestine/Palestinian, 119; educa-
tion, 57, 59–62, 70, 110–11;
manpower 34–5, 39–43,
50–1, 53, 57, 59–60, 62, 70,
110; political movements, 41,
43, 53, 60, 123; women,
34–5, 60
Palestine Liberation Organization,
41, 43, 60, 123
Pan-Arab Nationalism, 53–4
Patai, Raphael, 2
pearl-diving, 4–7
Pelly, Lewis, 4, 116
Persia *see* Iran
Personal Statute Law, 102
PFLP *see* Popular Front for the
Liberation of Palestine
Planning Board, 57
Planning Institute *see* Arab
Planning
PLO *see* Palestine Liberation
Organization
politics, 119, 121: Arab nationa-
list, 53–4; and discrimination,
46; and economic development,

93–4; education in, 63, 68; and
immigration, 34–8; and manpower planning, 103–6; and
middle class, 53–4; and women,
103–6
Popular Front for the Liberation
of Palestine 53, 123
population: age of, 12–15, 88,
114; composition of, 11–12;
growth of, 11–16, 29, 51–2,
114; and labor force, 11–29,
88–9, 107, 119; *see also*
immigrants
press, freedom of, 33
prices *see* costs
private sector, 77–9, 98, 112–13
productivity, low, 29
professional manpower, 9, 21–3,
29; emigrant, 55; immigrant,
36, 41, 50

Radaifs, 5–6
Ramadan, 46; *see also* Islam
reform: of civil service, 89–94; of
education, xiv, 95–9, 122, 124;
of Nationality Law, 106–11,
114, 125
refugees, 34
retirement, early, 91–2
revenue *see* income
rights, lack of *see* discrimination
ruling class, 52

Saudi Arabia: manpower from,
32, 36, 39–41; students from,
61, 68; trade with, 4
Schultz, W., 56, 122
science education, 63, 68, 96
scientific occupations, 22–3
service industries, 19, 22–3, 41
'servitude, indentured', 45
Shah of Iran, 38
Shari Law, 51, 63, 68
Shawikh Training Center, 74
Shia sect, 1, 8
Siyabs, 5–6
skilled labor, 7, 9, 26, 41, 71–81,
83; *see also* labor force; manual
labor; manpower

slaves, 8
Smith, D., 52, 121
smuggling, 7
social barriers: to education, 68;
 to manual work, xiv, 2, 20,
 71–2, 75; to women's work,
 16; *see also* discrimination
social services, 15, 19, 32, 77,
 89; denied, 44, 55
social composition of society,
 52–3; *see also* manual work;
 middle class
social work, 36
socialism, 35, 38
socialization, 51
Socknat, J. A., 72, 122
Spain, 71
Spanish Oil Co., 79–80
speech, freedom of, 33
sport, discrimination in, 50
Stanford Research Unit, 44, 55,
 97, 115, 117, 120, 123–4
status, 75; *see also* social barriers
Stoakes, Frank, 109, 125
strikes, 46
students *see* education; graduates
Suni sect, 1
Sweden, 77
Syria/Syrian: education, 59, 61,
 70; manpower, 32, 34–5,
 39–40, 42–3, 51; women, 36

'Tabeeat Ameel', 24
Tawash, 4
tax, 32, 41, 43; *see also* income
teachers: immigrant, 24, 36, 50,
 57, 59–60, 62, 70–1; income
 of, 24, 60; Kuwaiti, 57, 59;
 numbers of, 58–9, 119; training
 of, 69–70, 86
technical education *see* education,
 vocational
technicians, 26, 29
Telecommunication Institute, 74,
 76
Terry, J., 105, 125
time of stay in Kuwait, 40
towns, 47–8, 52, 121
trade, 1, 3–8, 11–12, 76, 116

trade unions, 46
training: teacher, 69–70, 86;
 vocational, 65–8, 71–81,
 83, 97–9, 105, 123
transport, employment in, 19–20
trans-shipment, 4
tribes, 1–3, 8, 83, 108–9, 116
Tunisia, 57
turnover, labor, 106

underdeveloped country, Kuwait
 as, 25
under-utilization of manpower, 24
unemployment, 7, 9, 32–3, 35, 37
unskilled labor, 34, 43–4, 49;
 *see also* labor force; manpower;
 manual labor
United Arab Emirates, 41
United Kingdom: education in,
 62–3, 67, 71, 81; manpower
 from, 39–40, 80; and oil
 companies, 10, 38
United Nations, 12, 66, 105, 117
United States: education in,
 62–3, 67, 71, 81; emigration
 to, 109; manpower from, 71,
 109; oil companies from, 10,
 79–80
universities *see* education, higher;
 Kuwait University
University Council, 63
urbanization, 47–8, 52, 121
USSR, 67, 77
Utubi tribe, 1

Villiers, A., 7, 116
Vocational and Technical Education for Females, 74
Vocational Training of Labor, 72
vocational and technical education
 *see* education

wage differential, 31, 40
War, Arab-Israeli, 34
Water Resources Center, 74, 76
welfare *see* social services
Wellsted, J. R., 5, 116
women: discrimination against,
 16–18, 27, 101–6; and

women: (*cont.*)
  education, 27, 57, 60, 63–71, 74, 105–6, 125; illiterate, 84, 104–5; immigrant, 16–17, 34–6, 39, 60; liberation of, 51, 99; and manpower planning, 99–102; and politics, 103–6; role of 99; working, xiv, 16–17, 29, 66, 88, 99–105, 124–5
Women's Council, 113–14
Women's Cultural Society, 124
work permits, 32
working class, 120; *see also* manual labor
World Bank, 44, 47, 51

Yemen, manpower from, 32–3, 39–40
Yousseff, Nadia H., 103, 124

For Product Safety Concerns and Information please contact our EU
representative  GPSR@taylorandfrancis.com
Taylor & Francis Verlag GmbH, Kaufingerstraße 24, 80331 München, Germany

www.ingramcontent.com/pod-product-compliance
Lightning Source LLC
Chambersburg PA
CBHW050528270326
41926CB00015B/3124